D1114930

The View From the Train

The View From the Train

Cities and Other Landscapes

PATRICK KEILLER

VERSO
London • New York

First published by Verso 2013

1 3 5 7 9 10 8 6 4 2

Verso
UK: 6 Meard Street, London W1F 0EG
US: 20 Jay Street, Suite 1010, Brooklyn, NY 11201
www.versobooks.com

Verso is the imprint of New Left Books

ISBN-13: 978-1-78168-140-4

British Library Cataloguing in Publication Data
A catalogue record for this book is available from the British Library

Library of Congress Cataloging-in-Publication Data

Keiller, Patrick.
The view from the train : cities and other landscapes / by Patrick Keiller.
pages cm
ISBN 978-1-78168-140-4 (hardback)
1. London (England)–In motion pictures. 2. London (England)–In art.
3. Landscapes–Great Britain–In art. I. Title.
PN1995.9.L57K45 2013
791.43'09421–dc23
2013024703

Typeset in Garamond by Hewer UK Ltd, Edinburgh
Printed and bound by CPI Group (UK) Ltd, Croydon, CR0 4YY

Contents

Introduction

The View from the Train

In 1977, I embarked on a project identifying and photographing what I later came to call 'found' architecture. I had lived in London for ten years and was becoming familiar with the city's geography. Living near Parliament Hill, working in Clapham, teaching part-time in Walthamstow and visiting sites over much of south London, I travelled between all these places, often, by motorcycle, and on these and similar journeys had encountered a variety of buildings and other structures with striking architectural qualities that were, mostly, not the result of conventional architectural activity. I decided to celebrate my first decade in London by making 35mm colour transparencies of these buildings, and any others that I might notice. I saw them initially as possible models for architectural production, as early twentieth-century modernists regarded some industrial and other structures, but they also seemed to admit the possibility of a more inclusive transformation of everyday surroundings, and I began to think they might be subjects for cinematography.

In January 1978, the exhibition *Dada and Surrealism Reviewed* opened at the Hayward Gallery. In its catalogue, and more particularly in an article by Roger Cardinal, 'Soluble City: The Surrealist Perception of Paris', in *Surrealism and Architecture*, a special issue of *Architectural Design* that accompanied the exhibition,[1] I read about the Surrealists' adoption of various sites and structures in Paris in the 1920s. It seemed to me that my identification of sites in London

Demolition of cattle market shed, La Villette, Paris, September 1980

in the 1970s could be seen as something similar. I began to take my slide collection more seriously, and in the autumn of 1979 it was the starting point of a two-year postgraduate project in Peter Kardia's Department of Environmental Media at the Royal College of Art. After a difficult year confronting a previously overlooked lack of technique, I assembled a series of monochrome slides of landscapes photographed in France during the summer of 1980 and wrote a five-minute narration to accompany them. I made another five-minute photo-narrative with photographs of a tall

wall next to a car park on Wormwood Scrubs, behind the prison, and then, on a Sunday afternoon in December, set out to look for a possible camera subject that I had seen from a passing train, where I found a structure that prompted a film.

The first essay in this collection, 'The Poetic Experience of Townscape and Landscape', is from this period. It identifies the literature that informed the project, revisited when beginning to make another film, *London* (1994), ten years later. The last and most recent essay, 'Imaging', recalls the journey, in December 1980, to the first film's location, and Walter Benjamin's essay 'Surrealism', in which he identifies the revolutionary potential of 'everything we have experienced on mournful railway journeys . . . on godforsaken Sunday afternoons'.[2] While I was writing the narration for the film *Robinson in Ruins* (2010), I remembered that I had first seen the final destination of its exploratory journey from a passing train, so that I have produced, so far, a body of work that begins and ends with views from trains.

The second essay here was written in 1983, while I was editing a second film, *Norwood* (1984), 'photographed entirely in Norwood'. The essay added Thomas De Quincey's *Confessions of an English Opium-Eater* to the references assembled by its predecessor. During the rest of the decade, I was making or writing proposals for films, while teaching two or three days a week, and there were no more essays for some time. I made three more short films, the first of which was photographed in September 1983, on eight 100-foot rolls of 16mm monochrome negative, during a journey with my partner and sometime collaborator Julie Norris to Italy, via Belgium, Germany and Switzerland. This footage eventually became a third film, *The End* (1986), the model for all its successors in that it was the first in which narration was written for an already-edited montage. The previous two films had been assemblies of a few long takes for which it was fairly easy to write continuous narrative, but in *The End*, most of the camera subjects appear only briefly.

Its completion was delayed by an unrealised project for a film about the life and work of the architect Adolf Loos, conceived after another journey, to Czechoslovakia in 1984, where we had visited some little-known Loos buildings. This was the first of several projects for more 'serious' films in which I hoped to re-engage with architecture. It was a collaboration with Yehuda Safran, who had been one of my tutors at the RCA, and Stuart Hood, who had just produced a film about Dario Fo for Channel Four Television. While I had migrated from architecture to art, Yehuda had been travelling in the opposite direction, and was by then involved with the architecture journal *9H*.[3] With Wilfried Wang, one of the journal's co-founders, he was co-curator of an Arts Council exhibition *The Architecture of Adolf Loos* that was to open at the Museum of Modern Art in Oxford in October 1985. When we returned from Czechoslovakia, I had the idea I might be able to make a film to accompany the exhibition. The initial proposal attracted some development finance, but none of the likely institutional patrons could be persuaded to commission the film.

Another of these would-be scholarly projects was for a film about the *Devětsil*, the Czechoslovakian avant-garde of the 1920s, and would have accompanied an exhibition that we had seen, then in preparation, on a second visit to Czechoslovakia, to Prague, Brno and Bratislava, in 1986: a two-week British Council academic exchange to study Czechoslovakian modern architecture of the 1920s and '30s. I was interested to examine any relationship between Surrealism and architectural practice: although the Surrealists in Paris had been interested in urban space and architecture, none of them were architects, but the *Devětsil*, the precursor of Czech Surrealism, included several architects, among them Jaromír Krejcar (1895–1949), the designer of the Czechoslovak pavilion at the 1937 Paris World Exhibition. The history of Czech modernism was then still largely unknown in English-speaking countries;[4] I wrote an account of what we had seen, published with a selection of our photographs in *Building Design*,[5] and gave a copy of the *Devětsil* catalogue to David Elliott, the director of the Museum of Modern Art in Oxford, where the exhibition opened in March 1990. The proposal for the film was developed with Keith Griffiths, later the producer of *London*. I returned to Prague in April 1994, for a conference of which there are some traces in the essay 'Popular Science', written five years later.

I had completed *The End* in the summer of 1986. It was selected for the Edinburgh Film Festival; some drawings I had made as aids to writing the narration were included in a touring exhibition that opened at the Serpentine Gallery, and in 1987 Channel Four bought the UK television rights. It was followed by two competitively won commissions for short films co-funded by Channel Four, the second of which was made for the British Film Institute and led to the opportunity to develop *London* (1994).

London and its sequel, *Robinson in Space* (1997), found an audience among academics and other specialists, initially in schools of architecture and among geographers. This led to invitations to write for architectural and other publications, and was a kind of reconciliation with my earlier career, so that there was no longer any need to pursue projects for architectural documentaries, but rather a tendency to see the realised films as some kind of spatial research. *London*, presented as a study by a fictional researcher, Robinson, of the 'problem' of London, was based on and sometimes parodied ideas about what constitutes successful urban space that had been current in architectural discourse since the late 1970s.[6] In this respect the film did not say very much that had not been said already. Its novelty was perhaps more in the way it represented what we already knew. Its sequel, however, seemed to confirm the validity of exploratory film-making as a method of research. Both *London* and *Robinson in Space* had set out with a perception of economic failure, the result of a backward, specifically English capitalism; but in the second film, this gave way to an understanding that the UK's social and physical impoverishment was not a consequence of some inevitable 'decline', but of the successful operation of a particular economic system in the interests of those who own it. The 'problem' that the film had set out to examine was revealed as the result of political decisions that could be challenged.

I was anxious to emphasise this outcome of the project, and concerned that reviewers might interpret the film as an account of industrial decline, which they sometimes did, perhaps in accordance with their expectations. In autumn 1996, when *Robinson in Space* was practically complete, I began an essay in which I hoped to give a more detailed exposition of what I thought the film had demonstrated. I met one of the co-editors of a book, then in preparation, and he asked me to send him the completed essay. The book was eventually published in 2001 as *The Unknown City*, in which the essay[7] was grouped with contributions from Doreen Massey and Patrick Wright, my co-researchers in a later project.

By this time, I had adapted *Robinson in Space* as a book.[8] I continued to write, when asked, usually in connection with a current or previous project, until early 2007, when I began the work preliminary to *Robinson in Ruins* (2010). During this long interval, I was mostly occupied with a project about the likely future of the UK's housing stock and another, developed from it, that set out to examine the built environment more generally. The first of these involved the production of a film, *The Dilapidated Dwelling* (2000); the second the development of a navigable assembly of early topographical films (including many views from moving trains), a virtual landscape of circa 1900 which became the basis for a series of exhibitions.[9] Much of the writing arose from these two projects. The essays are arranged in the order in which they were written, which is not always that in which they were published, or of the projects they relate to. Some were written in response to requests and invitations from academic or cultural contexts in which I thought I would be largely unknown, so that I explained myself from the beginning, and as a result there is some repetition, especially of quoted texts, that I have not attempted to edit.

During the interval between the completion of *Robinson in Space* and the commencement of *Robinson in Ruins*, I sometimes mentioned or alluded to a semi-fictional body, the Robinson Institute, most explicitly in an essay of that name, in which I suggested I might be one of its employees. This Robinson Institute – there are at least two others – was conceived in July 1999 with the aim of continuing the work of the protagonist of *London* and *Robinson in Space*, there being then, it seemed, no possibility to make another film in which he might continue the work himself. Robinson had been first imagined in June 1990, and was deployed as a way of allowing the films' narrators to put forward ideas that one might entertain but would perhaps not wholeheartedly adopt. His name was borrowed from one of the two itinerants in Kafka's *Amerika*, though at the time I wrote that he had been born in Shropshire.

As a series, the essays accompany the evolution, since the late 1970s, of an idea most recently restated in an introductory text for an exhibition, also called *The Robinson Institute*, at Tate Britain in 2012,[10] beginning: 'The Robinson Institute aims to promote political and economic change by developing the transformative potential of images of landscape.' Thirty-five years earlier, I had set out with what was essentially the same aim, expressed slightly differently.

February 2013

1

The Poetic Experience
of Townscape and Landscape

The desire to transform the world is not uncommon, and there are a number of ways of fulfilling it. One of these is by adopting a certain subjectivity, aggressive or passive, deliberately sought or simply the result of a mood, which alters experience of the world, and so transforms it.

There is nothing particularly new or unusual about this. The subjectivity involved is that of the wandering daydreamer – Edgar Allan Poe's in 'The Man of the Crowd'; Baudelaire's *flâneurs* and dandies; Apollinaire's Baron d'Ormesan, the inventor of amphionism; Louis Aragon and his contemporaries in *Le Paysan de Paris*. The thrill they all seek is the frisson Aragon termed 'a feeling for nature', their realm is the street, and the common object of their speculation the phenomenon of place.

I began to pursue the 'feeling for nature' several years ago. My starting point was that of an architect, and my motivation the desire to find, already existing, the buildings that I wanted to build but for a number of reasons was unable to.

The more I looked the more I found, and the more I found the more I looked, but gradually my interest shifted from the instant

Coal hopper, Nine Elms Lane, London SW8, 1979

transformation of a building (object), to the discovery of a deeper sensation of place (space) akin to the *stimmung* that Nietzsche discovered during his last euphoria in Turin, and that so affected de Chirico.

The present-day *flâneur* carries a camera and travels not so much on foot as in a car or on a train. There are several reasons for this, mostly connected with the decline of public life and urbanism (another kind of *flâneur* lives on in fiction – the private investigator – though his secrets are well hidden behind the street fronts), but also because there is something about a photograph or a shot in a film that exactly corresponds to the frisson that Aragon identified. As early as 1918, in his first published writing, he wrote: 'Likewise on the screen objects that were a few moments ago sticks of furniture or books of cloakroom tickets are transformed to the point where they take on menacing or enigmatic meanings.'[1]

I became a sort of architectural photographer and film-maker, trying to produce photographs and film footage that interpreted the objects of my desire as I saw them. It occurred to me that a common aspect of these interpretations was a kind of analogy that saw the places I 'discovered' and photographed in terms of other places that I knew, or knew of, and it also occurred to me that much of this experience of other places was gained from looking at photographs and films. The image of a place on the screen is transformed in exactly the same way as the objects to which Aragon refers – by the photography itself, by the images that precede and follow it, and by the narrative.

To a certain extent, I began to look at places as potential photographs, or better still, film images, and even the still photographs took on the character of film stills.

This visual material deliberately depicts places that are nearly or altogether devoid of human presence and activity, but which because of this absence are suggestive of what could happen, or what might have happened. They are places in which events might *take place*, and the events are seen rather as possible contemporary myths. But the myths have a history – maybe they *are* history – and this history can be constructed as a narrative – a reconstruction of a past daydream or the construction of a new one – which links still images or provides a setting for the film, in the same way as the locations provide a setting for the action in other films. The aim is to depict the place as some sort of historical palimpsest, and/or the corollary of this, an exposition of a state of mind.

Such is a summary of the development of this activity up to now. What follows is an attempt to map out the tradition that has supported this development. There are different aspects to this: the literature of the wandering daydreamer, whom I perhaps inaccurately term the *flâneur*; the visual arts tradition of the reinterpretation of everyday objects and landscapes, which might be termed Surrealist realism, though it probably has more to do with photography as a way of seeing than any particular mode of thought; and a way of depicting places in literature and film where they are inextricably bound up with the state of mind of the characters who inhabit or observe them.

The *Flâneur*

The *flâneur* as a literary motif appears in two modes, or rather can be seen as signifying two types of experience. The first of these is that of a wanderer, perhaps a dandy, who takes the city as his salon, strolling from café to bar in search of amusement and perhaps romance. His chance encounters are largely with people; his haunts chosen for the company they provide, rather than any melancholy architectural quality, and the oneiric quality of his experience is largely the result of his surrender to the randomness of urban life.

The other type of *flâneur* drifts through the city as if it were the substance of a dream, marvelling at the transformations that this brings about. He may meet others, he may fall passionately in love, but this is not his motive, it merely enhances his experience by enabling it to be shared.

There is also the lonely life of the street photographer, who acts the *flâneur* in the hope of recording little glimpses of the marvellous with his camera. His is a difficult task, for poetic insights so rarely survive their capture on the emulsion. But I digress.

Edgar Allan Poe wrote, in 1840, a short story, 'The Man of the Crowd'. The narrator, a convalescent, sits in a coffee house in London observing the thronging pedestrians passing the window. With that new vision often granted to those recently recovered from illness, he is enjoying finding distinct types among the passersby, when an old man who fits none of these captivates his curiosity. He leaves the coffee house and follows the man as he wanders through the streets with no aim other than to be constantly in a crowd. The afternoon turns to evening, and the evening to night. Still the old man walks on and still the narrator follows fascinated, trying to discover what the old man is about. On the evening of the following day he gives up his pursuit, knowing that it will never end: '"This old man," I said at length, "is the type and the genius of deep crime. He refuses to be alone. *He is the man of the crowd.*"'

While Poe's attitude to the old man is far from any sympathetic identification, here I believe for the first time we see some recurring themes in 'urban dream' writing: the narrator's convalescent state, a heightened state of awareness: 'one of those happy moods which are so precisely the converse of *ennui* – moods of the keenest appetency, when the film from the mental vision departs'[2] – and his resultant rather alienated observation through the window of what came to be called 'modern life'; his subsequent pursuit of an enigma; the description of the streets through which they pass, the low-life – they enter a gin-palace at dawn – and above all the emerging sensitivity to the erotic implications of crowds.

Poe's reputation in Europe was considerably enhanced by Baudelaire, who praised and translated his works. He quotes 'The Man of the Crowd' in 'The Painter of Modern Life'. Baudelaire's writing is full of awareness of 'the poetry of modern life', the life of the streets and boulevards and other public places, but specific references to townscape are rare. His encounters are with people, or spirits, but not places. In the letter to Arsène Houssaye, which serves as the preface to *Paris Spleen*, he writes of his desire to create the poetic prose of which the book is composed: 'It was, above all, out of my exploration of huge cities, out of the medley of their innumerable interrelations, that this haunting ideal was born.'[3]

Apollinaire produced the most demonstrative of *flâneur* writings. In *The Wandering Jew* the story is not unlike 'The Man of the Crowd', but here the enigma guides the narrator through Prague until it transpires that he is several centuries old.

The most prophetic of Apollinaire's stories here is 'The False Amphion', one of the *Stories and Adventures of Baron d'Ormesan*.[4] The Baron is an old acquaintance of the narrator, who thinks he is a tourist guide, but the Baron, on the contrary, has invented a new art form, amphionism:

> 'The instrument of this art, and its subject matter, is a town of which one explores a part in such a way as to excite in the soul of the amphion, or neophyte, sentiments that inspire in them a sense

of the sublime and the beautiful, in the same way as music, poetry
and so on . . .'

'But,' I said laughingly, 'I practice amphionism every day. All I
have to do is go for a walk . . .'

'Monsieur Jourdain,' cried Baron d'Ormesan, 'what you say is
perfectly true! You practice amphionism without knowing it.'

Now this is all very ironic, but the irony is directed not at the idea
of poetic wandering, but at the Baron's insistence that the art
consists of composing the journeys, rather than on the one hand
building the buildings, or on the other concretising the poetic experience of wandering among them – in other words, that the art
depended on the sensibility of the artist, not what he did with it.
The Baron's adventures are full of similar misunderstandings, such
as the film-makers who, for the sake of realism in their film, pay a
man to actually murder a couple.

The point about subjective transformations of townscape is that
they do depend on a certain state of mind, which can be adopted
deliberately (this is why I write of 'aggressive' subjectivity), but not
by an audience (and probably best not at all, for it is best to take
one's reveries as they come).

Tourism

This was certainly the case on 14 April 1921, the date of the first
Surrealist event. Organised by André Breton, it was to consist solely
of direct experience of the city. The Surrealists had already explored
brothels and the 'cretinous suburbs' as well as the flea market, but
they had not yet demonstrated their discoveries to the public.

The new itinerary would 'put in unison the unconscious of the
city with the unconscious of men', and was to take in St Julien-le-
Pauvre, the Parc des Buttes-Chaumont, the Gare St Lazare and the
Canal de l'Ourcq. The first expedition, advertised throughout Paris,
to St Julien-le-Pauvre, was a complete failure. It rained and no tourists turned up, and the rest of the tours were cancelled.[5]

It was more than thirty years before anyone tried anything like this again. Once more in Paris, in the early 1950s, the Lettrist group developed the techniques of 'drifting' and 'psychogeography'. Drifting was a free-association in space. Drifters would follow the streets, go down alleys, through doors, over walls, up trees – anywhere that they found desirable. Later 'mass drifts' involved teams linked by walkie-talkie radio. Psychogeography was the correlation of the material obtained by drifting. It was used in making 'emotional maps' of parts of the city, and in other ways.

In 1958, the Lettrists evolved into the Situationist International, and in 1968 their polemic was influential in *les événements*. Drifting was still a preoccupation. In *Ten Days That Shook the University*, an account of the election and subsequent propagandist exploits of a Situationist-inspired group who in 1966 gained a short-lived control of the students' union of Strasbourg University, there is a strip cartoon of two cowboys riding through a landscape:

'What's your scene man?' asks one.

'Reification,' the other replies.

'Yeah? I guess that means pretty hard work with big books and piles of paper on a big table.'

'Nope. I drift. Mostly I just drift.'[6]

Drifting, it seems, has reconstituted itself as a myth.

Le Paysan de Paris

Louis Aragon began writing *Le Paysan de Paris* in 1924, three years after the ill-fated touristic event. It is constructed about descriptions of two places: the Passage de l'Opera, in whose bars he and his contemporaries drank and talked, and the Parc des Buttes-Chaumont, which they held in high esteem as an oneiric location, and which was to have been the subject of one of the touristic ventures. Between the two descriptions, he outlines the genesis of 'a feeling for nature':

I felt the great power that certain places, certain sights exercised over me, without discovering the principle of this enchantment. Some everyday objects unquestionably contained for me a part of that mystery, plunged me into that mystery . . . The way I saw it, an object became transfigured: it took on neither the allegorical aspect nor the character of the symbol, it did not so much manifest an idea as constitute that very idea. Thus it extended deeply into the world's mass . . . I acquired the habit of constantly referring the whole matter to the judgement of a kind of frisson which guaranteed the soundness of this tricky operation.[7]

I have already compared this frisson to that preceding the click of a camera, but Aragon's account of his discovery outlines a way of looking at things that runs through the whole history of twentieth-century art, and twentieth-century attitudes to pre-twentieth-century art. On the next page he looks at petrol pumps: 'The nameless sculptors who erected these metallic phantoms were incapable of conforming to a living tradition like that which traced the cruci-form shapes of churches. These modern idols share a parentage that makes them doubly redoubtable.'[8]

Petrol pumps like these turn up in the paintings of Edward Hopper – *Gas* (1940) and *Four Lane Road* (1956) – and in the photographs of Robert Frank – *The Americans* (1958). Similar perceptions of everyday objects occur in painting, sculpture, photography and film in areas as diverse as metaphysical painting, *film noir* or 'conceptual' art, never mind pop art. The transforma-tion may be seen both as a realisation of the ontologically miraculous and as a hysterical alienation from banality. What is remarkable about Aragon's transformation is not just that he managed to perform it without benefit of nostalgia, which so automatically provides a poetic cloak for any object (those petrol pumps, or their heads, also turn up highly priced in antique shops), but that he managed to direct it at whole districts of the city. André Breton said of him, years after their break: 'I still recall the extraordinary role that Aragon played in our daily strolls through Paris. The localities that we passed through in his

Jacques-André Boiffard: 'My point of departure will be the Hôtel des Grands Hommes . . .' from *Nadja* (1928). The statue, melted down during the occupation, was of Jean-Jacques Rousseau.

company, *even the most colourless ones* [my emphasis], were positively transformed by a spellbinding romantic inventiveness.'[9]

Breton, for whom the street was 'the fountain of all true experience', wrote another classic text of Surrealist Paris, the story of his relationship with the enigmatic, innocent, experienced Nadja. An account of Surrealist love (shared revelation rather than physical passion), their affair takes place in the streets, in cafés, on trains. Some of these locations are illustrated by a number of remarkably prosaic photographs.

The eroticism portrayed is as much that of their relationship with their surroundings as with each other. Georges Bataille writes: 'Erotic activity, by dissolving the separate beings that participate in it, reveals their fundamental continuity, like the waves of a stormy sea.'[10]

Love is the conquest of the discontinuity between individuals: hence the erotic dimension to 'losing oneself in the crowd', or indeed losing oneself in the city, habitually so alienating, reconstituted instead as a dream. It is in such an appropriation, such a repossession of townscape – or landscape – that the possibility of an erotic relationship between people and public space is to be found.[11]

There are other Surrealist townscape texts: Robert Desnos's *La Liberté ou l'Amour!* (1927) and those of Walter Benjamin, notably *Marseilles* (1928), in which he converts the then new cathedral into a railway station, and *Hashish in Marseilles* (1928), which enjoys the transformations enabled by the drug.[12]

Benjamin recounts the remark made of Eugène Atget that he photographed the deserted Paris streets 'like scenes of crime': 'The scene of a crime, too, is deserted; it is photographed for the purpose of establishing evidence. With Atget, photographs become standard evidence for historical occurrences, and acquire a hidden political significance.'[13]

Bernard Tschumi has written that, for Georges Bataille, 'architecture covers the scene of the crime with monuments'[14] (this is perfectly true – just think of Trafalgar Square). Atget's depictions of public places in and around Paris captured, in the most modest way (this is surely his strength), the sense that 'anything could happen' that the Surrealists were later to write about, as well as being evidence of all the terrible things that already had happened. They reveal an ambiguity, a potential for transformations both subjective and actual, in ordinary locations. The crime that Bataille and Benjamin allude to is an ambiguous affair, but its major resonance is that of the rarity, in everyday experience and in actuality, of such transformations. They come about only, if ever, in reveries, revolutions, or the more poignant moments of war.

Atget's photographs were of the streets; Surrealist photographers went to more exotic locations. Eli Lotar's photographs of the abattoirs at La Villette illustrate Bataille's entry 'abattoir' in the section 'Chronique: Dictionnaire' in *Documents*.[15] Bataille concerns himself with outlining the significance of abattoirs, that they are the modern counterpart of sacrificial temples in which animals were killed for both religious and alimentary purposes, the cursed status of abattoirs in modern times resulting from the denial of their religious function. Lotar's photographs demonstrate this world within the one we think we know, as they demonstrate the camera's ability to unmask it. It is almost as if the machine was built for this purpose, as we now know only too well, for indiscriminate transformations of the ordinary into the miraculous now form one of the mainstays of advertising.

Anguish

At the same time, the discovery of the ability to perceive the marvellous leads to the discovery that things have a habit of not staying that way:

> Although I can always see how beautiful anything could be if only I could change it, in practically every case there is nothing I can really do. Everything is changed into something else in my imagination, then the dead weight of things changes it back into what it was

in the first place. A bridge between imagination and reality must be built.[16]

In Poe's writing, taken as a whole, two things seem to stand out as most remarkable: his descriptions of extraordinary states of consciousness, and of rooms, buildings and landscapes. Many of his works consist of little else: 'The Philosophy of Furniture', a treatise on decor; 'The Domain of Arnheim' and its 'pendant' 'Landor's Cottage', which describe respectively the creation of a superlative landscape garden by an individual of exemplary endowments, and an idyllic cottage inhabited by an idyllic couple in an idyllic setting. There is no other purpose to these works than these descriptions. In 'The Pit and the Pendulum', the greater part of the writing is description of the narrator's delirium as he hovers on the edge of consciousness, and most of the rest details his gradual awareness of the awful particularities of the dungeon into which he has been cast. In 'The Fall of the House of Usher', the place and the state of mind of its residents are even more inextricably bound up, though not this time in the first person, for the narrator is a guest: 'I know not how it was – but, with the first glimpse of the building, a sense of insufferable gloom pervaded my spirit. I say insufferable; for the feeling was unrelieved by any of that half-pleasurable, because poetic, sentiment, with which the mind usually receives even the sternest natural images of the desolate or terrible.'

With this observation, Poe distances the narrator from the reader, who cannot help imagine some 'poetic' gloom precisely because it will only exist in his imagination. Poe is pinpointing a rather photographic dilemma – for photographs of unpoetic gloom, provided they are good photographs, generally make it look rather poetic whether this is the intention or not, as in war reportage and so on. The narrator goes on: 'I looked upon the scene before me . . . with an utter depression of soul which I can compare to no earthly sensation more properly than to the after-dream of the reveller upon opium – the bitter lapse into everyday life – the hideous dropping off of the veil.'[17]

Here he compares a particular state of mind with that following the loss of another, again a kind of paradox. But this is typical, for Poe is at his best when describing not just the heightened states of mind of his characters, but the anguish which their (and presumably his) sensibilities bring about in their everyday lives. Thus, of Roderick Usher:

> He suffered much from a morbid acuteness of the senses; the most insipid food was alone endurable; he could wear only garments of certain texture; the odours of all flowers were oppressive; his eyes were tortured by even a faint light; and there were but peculiar sounds, and these from stringed instruments, which did not inspire him with horror.[18]

Throughout Poe's work, there is an implication that those who have access to heightened states of awareness are bound to suffer. Delirium is the result of illness or injury ('The Pit and the Pendulum', 'The Oval Portrait'), persons of extreme sensibility suffer ('Usher'), are haunted by irrational fears ('The Premature Burial'), or turn to drink and murder ('The Black Cat'), and those who cultivate the senses in the face of suffering and adversity invite destruction nonetheless ('The Masque of the Red Death'). He seems especially familiar, like the narrator in 'Usher', with the depression encountered when any heightened state departs.

This is a recurring theme in Baudelaire. In 'The Double Room', one of the prose poems of *Paris Spleen*, the room is an idyllic space; the light, the furnishings and the company are sublime, but then little memories of current circumstances alter this perception: 'And that perfume out of another world which in my state of exquisite sensibility was so intoxicating? Alas, another odour has taken its place, of stale tobacco mixed with nauseating mustiness. The rancid smell of desolation.'[19] There is a political dimension to this:

> Each subjectivity is different from every other one, but all obey the same will to self-realisation. The problem is one of setting their variety in a common direction, of creating a united front of subjectivity. Any attempt to build a new life is subject to two conditions:

firstly, that the realisation of each individual subjectivity will either take place in a collective form or it will not take place at all; and, secondly, that 'To tell the truth, the only reason anyone fights is for what they love. Fighting for everyone else is only the consequence' (Saint-Just).[20]

Transformations of everyday space are subjective, but they are not delusions, simply glimpses of what could happen, and indeed does happen at moments of intense collectivity, during demonstrations, revolutions and wars. It is this realisation, together with that of the individual's predicament, 'his desperate desire to flee from the prison of his subjectivity, his furious longing to find some escape from the ugliness of modem life',[21] that set up a dialectic that can inform an outlook on the townscape and landscape that constitute our surroundings, which are, as Georges Bataille points out, the physiognomy of our society.[22]

2

Atmosphere, Palimpsest and Other Interpretations of Landscape

I don't suppose I can have missed a single episode in the first year of *Z Cars*, but I can't remember any of them. In fact I don't think I can remember in detail anything that I ever saw on television apart from a few oft-repeated items, and I suspect that such lack of retention is general.

This is a pity, for apparently only two episodes of *Z Cars* survive from the first six months of the series. I mention this having seen them (again?) at the NFT last September, this time on the cinema screen, where they were revealed as examples of a hitherto unknown and rather timeless genre. (Although there were elements of nostalgia: the cars, for instance – there were always an awful lot of Fords. Perhaps the BBC had done a deal.)

'They fight crime on wheels in a new series beginning tonight', said the *Radio Times* on 28 December 1961. Fighting crime on wheels has got itself a bad name in the period since, but in those days the lads in the cars were cast as more or less sophisticated social workers, imbued albeit with the extra moral authority of the law, who cruised from domestic disturbance to truant shoplifter distributing a positive understanding over the public-sector suburban desolation of (Kirkby) Newtown. It is this desolation that hasn't dated: it's all still there, and it still appears on television, in the work of Alan Bleasdale et al., though for my money a low-key *Z Cars* beats their didactic tear-jerking any day. The difference is that in 1961 things were considered to be capable of getting better, whereas now every-one thinks they're getting worse. Both the episodes shown took a 'social problem' as their theme rather than any crime. The first had Jock Weir and Fancy Smith ('Z Victor 1') trying to prevent the biggest of a shipload of hard-drinking just-got-paid Norwegian whalers from being fleeced by a girl desperate for money (the 'social problem'), posing as a waterfront prostitute. All the action takes place inside a pub, which is just as well as the surviving print is re-filmed from a video monitor and is not very sharp.

The other episode ('People's Property', 15 May 1962) was mostly the original, probably 35mm, film, but parts of this have evidently gone missing and been replaced by sections re-filmed from a video monitor, which are inserted quite uninhibitedly, the change often occurring in mid-scene. The original photography is very good, and when seen on the screen is reminiscent of later Ealing films. This is an observation one could never make seeing it on television, and which quite undermined my vague memories of the series. The episode makes 'much use of atmospheric locations', which proba-bly also did not come across on television, the landscape locations suffering most of all. It is not, however, my intention to make a polemic on television versus cinema or video versus film, by suggesting that revelatory experience when seeing a twenty-one-year-old television programme in the cinema is proof that, at least as regards the meaningful portrayal of landscape, television is a medium deeply inferior to the cinema. I probably do think all these things, but my purpose is rather to use the episode as a vehicle with which to get from the desolate landscape of Kirkby to another.

The story follows the exploits of two boys (the 'social problem'), one a clever misfit, one his stooge. The former looks a bit like John Lennon aged ten, but we weren't to know that then. First discovered misbehaving on the roof of a factory at night (the first atmospheric location), they go on to shoplifting and handbag theft. They are caught, but let out again because all the places they could be sent are full up. Skipping school, they go on a spree of petty theft until they are caught again but let out for the same reason as before. In a last gesture they run away to Wales to climb a mountain, departing on the bus to Wrexham via the Mersey Tunnel. Jock and Fancy (ZV1 again) find out about this shortly after the bus has emerged from the tunnel, but being some miles behind, don't catch up with it until the boys have been thrown off as a result of their unruly behaviour, and hitched a lift with a farmer in a Ford Zephyr. He lets them off at his gate and they continue on foot up the desired mountain. By the time Jock and Fancy arrive they have left the road and are halfway up. J and F leg it up the hill, and after a display of puffing and rugby skills they apprehend the pair. All this time they have been facing in one direction, in single-minded pursuit of their respective goals, but after the capture, seemingly accepted by the boys, they all turn round, having got their breath back only to have it taken away again by a view for twenty miles across the Dee valley. 'By 'eck,' gasps Fancy, touched by the sublime, 'look at THAT.' The camera obliges with a slow pan over the view, during which not a word is spoken. An awesome spectacle of landscape, it seems, transcends even the most difficult predicament.

This is even more true in films than in life, and in both realms of experience such sentiments are prone to cliché. What is more surprising is that they seem to be universally felt, and to a great extent in the same way by persons of widely differing political and other persuasions, whereas other manifestations of beauty often are not. There is nothing improbable in the idea of a policeman, even a real policeman lacking the insight of Fancy Smith, being struck dumb by a good view.

The view itself is worthy of some scrutiny: a patchwork of fields and hedges, the occasional tree or copse, the ground undulating in a small way, all this viewed from high ground to the west and lit from behind the viewer by the afternoon sun. This is a dairy-farming landscape like those featured in butter commercials. It belongs to that type of view that could properly be called 'green and pleasant land', and is the dominant image of English landscape. In fact it is found only in small parts of the country to the west of a line between London and, say, Lancaster. The eastern counties and the hilly districts are not a part of this arcadia, and tend to be seen either as local phenomena, or in terms of landscapes of other countries: the East Riding of Yorkshire is 'middle European', the Cotswolds 'Mediterranean'.

The Dee valley view is analogous with the view across the Severn valley from Malvern, perhaps that from Hergest Ridge, and others in the west of England. I suspect, however, that the hegemony of this type of view in the national imagination has more to do with the former appearance of Sussex than anything else, and reflects the class status of the home counties: their arcadia an imagined former rural identity now undermined by middle-distance commuting and suburbanisation. The famous view through the gap in the trees that surround the Duke of Norfolk's cricket ground at Arundel Castle is surviving evidence for this supposition, and its connotations are in this location pinpointed by the feudal sounds of leather on willow and so on.

The society of the Dee valley is very much that of the Cheshire 'county'. It is their creation, in as much as all landscape is the result of human interference. It is where the Cheshire hunt still hunts, now with the support of non-landed bourgeois money from nearby metropolitan areas. In short, the connotations of both its imagery and its inhabitants are more or less disgraceful, and yet its representation remains moving. The experience of landscape not only transcends individual suffering (the boys' capture), but even that very general tragedy of which the landscape itself is a result.

This combination of the tragic and the euphoric is a dominant quality in innumerable depictions of landscape, especially when these are from above, and so supply implications of pattern, understanding or explanation, and hence compassion not available to observers on the ground.

It is a view that probably dates only from the nineteenth century, and is in any case not universal. Notwithstanding the difference in motive, those paintings of various of Napoleon's battles, seen from a nearby hill, contrast with battle scenes from a similar viewpoint in *Birth of a Nation*. The paintings display a disciplined efficiency, while Griffith, with a comparable lack of technical sophistication in visual matters, manages to present his war in a far more complex picture of chaos, squalor and pain.

Daniel Defoe, writing in 1724, says of the Dee valley: 'The soil is extraordinary good, and the grass they say, has a peculiar richness in it, which disposes the creatures to give a great quantity of milk, and that very sweet and good.'[1]

Already the butter commercial is imminent, but here beauty is synonymous, rather than simultaneous, with productivity or prosperity. In any case Defoe may be said to pre-date the sense of the picturesque. In the rare instances where he describes landscape itself, that of the Yorkshire Dales for instance, his purpose is to discuss the disposition of industry upon it.[2] For him the Lake District was a barren wasteland.

In Richard Wilson's painting *Holt Bridge on The River Dee* (before 1762), the picturesque is already well established, not so much a result of easier travel or burgeoning industrialisation, but the concurrent desire for a Virgilian idyll in which to set the then present-day. In the painting, which echoes a Venetian sensibility as well as that of Claude, elements of the scenery are stressed for their classical comparability: the

Courtesy of the National Gallery

Richard Wilson, *Holt Bridge on the River Dee* (before 1762)

sandstone cliff; the (church) tower; the flat plain and distant hills; the 'peasants' and the bridge. All these elements are interpreted in terms of Wilson's repertoire of elements of classical *mise-en-scène* collected in his sketchbooks while in Italy. Most important, because invisible, is the historical significance of the bridge itself as the link between England and Wales, and the aura of antiquity which this bestows.

This metaphorical transposition of landscape – seeing somewhere as somewhere else – and the consequent effect on the landscape are widely encountered in art, life and the relations between these. In the simplest sense, in Chris Petit's *Radio On* (1979), photographed by Martin Schäfer, the journey along the A4 is converted by the cinematography into one across some unspecified but definitely East European plain. Blea Tarn, which lies at the top of a pass between the two Langdale valleys in the Lake District, was the inspiration and subject of a passage in Wordsworth's *The Excursion*. A later sensibility, aroused perhaps by Wordsworth's poem, but informed more by Chinese and Japanese scenes, was inspired in the unknown landscape-gardening landowner who planted rhododendrons around the tarn, which still thrive despite the altitude, and parallel the domestication of Wordsworth's vision. This is not so much 'seeing somewhere as somewhere else', but 'seeing somewhere in terms of a picture of somewhere else'.

By the time Thomas De Quincey passed through the Dee Valley, he too a runaway schoolboy in 1802, the sensibility of Wilson's generation had had its effect:

> The Vale of Gressford, for instance . . . offered a lovely little seclusion . . . But this did not offer what I wanted. Everything was elegant, polished, quiet, throughout the lawns and groves of this verdant retreat: no rudeness was allowed here; even the little brooks were trained to 'behave themselves'; and the two villas of the reigning ladies . . . showed the perfection of good taste. For both ladies had cultivated a taste for painting.[3]

The last sentence tells all. De Quincey moved on into the mountains in rehearsal for his sojourn as the Wordsworths' neighbour at Grasmere. Earlier in the same journey, he pinpoints the phenomenon:

> an elaborate and pompous sunset hanging over the mountains of North Wales. The clouds passed slowly through several arrangements, and in the last of these I read the very scene which six months before I had read in a most exquisite poem of Wordsworth's . . . The scene in the poem ('Ruth'), that had been originally mimicked by the poet from the sky, was here re-mimicked and rehearsed to the life, as it seemed, by the sky from the poet.[4]

Poe was familiar with this mechanism of romanticisation, but such ephemeral effects do not satisfy him: the landscape gardener is produced to cement the cyclical relationship between poetic experience and the material world, to conduct

> 'its adaption to the eyes which were to behold it on earth': in his explanation of this phraseology, Mr Ellison did much toward solving what has always seemed to me an enigma: — I mean the fact (which none but the ignorant dispute) that no such combination of scenery exists in nature as the painter of genius may produce. No such paradises are to be found in reality as have glowed on the canvas of Claude. In the most enchanting of natural landscapes there will always be found a defect or an excess . . . In all other matters we are justly instructed to regard nature as supreme . . . In landscape alone is the principle of the critic true.[5]

The supposition may be said to rest on misconceptions, but in the end it probably holds true. Landscapes that do not result from human intervention – rain forests, uninhabited islands – are no less susceptible to criticism than those that do, and still life and portraiture generally involve a far greater degree of verisimilitude, and consequently less idealisation, than depictions of landscape. The relation between the idea and the reality of landscape really is different.

The reasons for this lie in the rather obvious distinction between, say, a sheep, as a thing, and a landscape, as perhaps also a thing, but more usefully a general disposition of things (one of which may be the sheep), and in the further distinction between the relationship of a viewer and the sheep, objects of more or less equal status, and that between this viewer and the landscape, in which the viewer and the sheep are constituents in the general disposition.

In the first distinction, the general disposition of things is much more susceptible to alteration (landscape gardening) than any single thing (the sheep), and is corollary-wise much more likely to be at variance with any imagination of it (a picture) than would be the case with the sheep. Thus the possibility of and the desire for landscape gardening both stem in the very same way from the nature of landscape itself, and the cyclical relationship between the imagination of it and its reality is permitted: the real appearance of Tuscany gives rise to an imagination of landscape which gives rise to an alteration of the real appearance of England. This relationship is not confined to visual matters: every landscape has its myth and every myth has its history. The landscape of Milton Keynes is rooted in a myth about Los Angeles, and the landscape of suburbia ('unplanned') is rooted in a myth about yeoman-villagers and their village, folk memory of the English petty bourgeois.

In the second distinction, the viewer's gaze surrounds the sheep: it is apprehended all at once. Even if the sheep were as big as a house, the viewer would only have to move away from it to restore the relationship. (If it *were* a house, the position would be slightly different, as the inside could not readily be apprehended, and when it could, the viewer would be inside *it* and only partly aware of the outside. This is the unique dual status of architecture.)

In the landscape, however, the viewer is always surrounded, and so the business of picturing is infinitely more complex both technically and conceptually. Devices such as the 'frame within the frame' have evolved partly to deal with this, and it is this distinction between modes of viewing that differentiates the parallel analogies between an object and an idea, and between one's surroundings and a mood, atmosphere or state of mind.

Landscape functions in all these ways in the cinema, perhaps more so than anywhere else. The tragic–euphoric palimpsest; the reciprocity of imagination and reality; place seen in terms of other place; setting as a state of mind – all are phenomena that coincide in films.

The exact way in which this happens is generally determined by a more or less complex and more or less intense metaphorical relationship between landscape and narrative, like that between the volcano and Ingrid Bergman's spiritual crisis in *Stromboli*. The volcano, as singular a presence as any, is employed in a variety of ways: its rumblings parallel her unease; it is the cause of her isolation and it hosts her despair and redemption when she tries to climb over it to the outside world.

Similar ambiguities between benevolence and malevolence are general and twofold. The landscape may or may not be sympathetic to the protagonists, and the film may or may not echo this judgement. In Herzog's South American ventures both forest and invaders are equally godforsaken, but the forest is bound to win, and few tears are to be shed over this. On the other hand, the geography of *The Wages of Fear* is a lackey of the employers, and it really is sad when Yves Montand's truck goes over the edge.

In John Ford's films a more metaphorical idea of predicament is entertained. *The Lost Patrol* slowly and inexorably pursues the archetypal spiritual analogies of the desert, while the impotence of Boris Karloff's religious-fanatic behaviour increases as it becomes more extreme. Ford's desert is very like his opposite-but-similar ocean in *The Long Voyage Home*. In *The Quiet Man* the surface of Ireland is cast (as it often is) as a palimpsest of the type previously described, and the conflict that is the film's story is over rights of access to history and 'rootedness' through ownership of land and other property. The outsider, John Wayne, despite the local origin of his parents, is only able to secure these rights to their past by employing his skill as an ex-champion boxer, the very thing he was so anxious to conceal in his own past. Subject-matter and setting are even more closely identified in *The Grapes of Wrath*. Here the palimpsest is active, for the landscape itself, by physically blowing away, becomes the instrument by which the landowners' exploitation leads to suffering on a biblical scale.

With Renoir the relationship is similar, if more subtle. The passionate excesses of *La Bête Humaine* are orchestrated entirely by the railway, its own landscape and that through which it runs. The sexuality of the railway engine pervades the intricacy of timetabling, and the landscape, again as a palimpsest, models the ideas about heredity and misfortune that underlie Zola's novel. The country house and its surroundings in *La Règle du Jeu* offer some kind of social order, but it is riddled with pitfalls, like the location where the shooting party goes wrong, all marshes and thickets: a model for the confusion that is unleashed upon it. In *La Grande Illusion* the geography is again a predicament. The hostility of the warring nations and their frontiers are mocked by the continuity of landscape and its beauty, as in an atlas the physical map mocks its political partner. At the same time, for the escaping prisoner of war, topography is all-important: inaccessibility and concealment now offer safety rather than the peacetime risk of getting lost; and all the best frontiers are located by geographical features.

Invasion of the Body Snatchers shows a landscape which may offer concealment, required despite the lack of war, but is more likely to trip up running feet shod with city shoes. It conspires with the invaders to isolate the town without the need for frontiers, and lends its fertility to their market-gardening operation. In a paranoid time nature is at best inconvenient and at worst actively hostile. Civil engineering projects were the human revenge for this. In *Hell Drivers*, a pleasant enough countryside is subjugated to the needs of construction. The landscape is again physically involved in the story: the protagonists dig great holes in it, pick it up and carry it about. Their pitfalls are provided by the remains of previous human exploitations: the narrow twisting roads on which they drive so competitively, and the abandoned quarry pit, on the edge of which they fight.

Night of the Living Dead is perhaps more visually sensitive than some later films (*Zombies*, *Shivers*, *Rabid*, and so on) in which unpleasant beings confront living humans, and in which landscape generally plays a neutral role. The opening scenes show a country graveyard in a Pennsylvania landscape. This scene is well aware of its history: it looks European, and the name of Penn underlines this connection. Elegantly photographed in sylvan black and white – not at all *noir* – it presents a poetic if melancholy scene. Only its occupants are spiritually uneasy as they visit a grave, while the technological hubris of their society accidentally restores a kind of collective life to their recent dead, who rapidly infest the landscape, devouring the living where they find them.

Several of the still-living find themselves sharing the refuge of an isolated house as night falls. This idea of the solitary house in the landscape is very clear, almost archetypal, as in 'The Fall of the House of Usher'. The landscape itself remains neutral: it provides concealment but isolates the victims from rescue; the living dead blunder across it, but it offers the possibility of escape. This does not occur, though, and the greater part of the rest of the film is set inside the benighted house, and offers more elegant photography in an essay of architectural phenomenology worthy of Gaston Bachelard: inside and outside; upstairs, downstairs and basement; windows, doors, cupboards and furniture are all clearly differentiated by the acuteness of the unusual circumstances. In the morning the one survivor, a black man, emerges from the basement to be shot by a sheriff's posse, who assume he is just another living deadman, or by now simply don't care.

This brutalised attitude is duplicated in the portrayal of the landscape. Nothing about it has physically changed, but now the camera ceases to flatter: the sky is bleached, the composition blunt. There is an expediency like that of television news footage. The only feeling left is the uneasy camaraderie between the slobs who comprise the posse, and it is their view that we see in these last scenes. As always, the meaning in the landscape resides only in the imagination of whoever looks upon it.

3

Port Statistics

The following paragraphs were written in the last months of 1996, during the final stages of production of a film *Robinson in Space* (1997), for which the journeys they recall were carried out. Towards the end of a previous film, *London* (1994), its fictitious narrator offers the ambiguous assertion: 'The true identity of London . . . is in its absence . . .' 'Absence of what?' the viewer might ask. One of many possible answers to this question is that London came into being and grew as a port city. Its port activity is now largely *absent*, but continues somewhere else. One of *Robinson*'s objectives was to locate some of the economic activity that no longer takes place in cities.

Robinson in Space (1997) was photographed between March and November 1995. It documents the explorations of an unseen fictional character called Robinson, who was the protagonist of the earlier *London* (1994), a re-imagination of its subject suggested by the Surrealist literature of Paris. *Robinson in Space* is a similar study of the *look* of present-day England in 1995, and was suggested to some extent by Daniel Defoe's *Tour through the Whole Island of Great Britain* (1724–26). Among its subjects are many new spaces, particularly the sites where manufactured products are produced, imported and distributed. Robinson has been commissioned by 'a well-known international advertising agency' to undertake a study of the 'problem' of England.[1] It is not stated in the film what this problem is, but there are images of Eton, Oxford and Cambridge, a Rover car plant, the inward investment sites of Toyota and Samsung, a lot of ports, supermarkets, a shopping mall, and other subjects which evoke the by now familiar critique of 'gentlemanly capitalism', which sees the UK's economic weakness as a result of the City of London's long-term (English) neglect of the (United Kingdom's) industrial economy, particularly its manufacturing base.

Early in the film, its narrator quotes from Oscar Wilde's *The Picture of Dorian Gray*: 'It is only shallow people who do not judge by appearances. The true mystery of the world is the visible, not the invisible.'[2] The appearances by which the viewer is invited to judge are initially the dilapidation of public space, the extent of visible poverty, the absence of UK-branded products in the shops and on the roads, *and* England's cultural conservatism. Robinson's image of the UK's industry is based on his memories of the collapse of the early Thatcher years. He has assumed that poverty and dilapidation are the result of economic failure, and that economic failure is a result of the inability of UK industry to produce *desirable* consumer products. He believes, moreover, that this has something to do with the *feel* of 'Middle England', which he sees as a landscape increasingly characterised by sexual repression, homophobia and the frequent advocacy of child-beating. At the same time, he is dimly aware that the United Kingdom is still the fifth-largest trading economy in the world and that British – even English people, particularly women and the young – are probably neither as sexually unemancipated, as sadistic or as miserable as he thinks the *look* of the UK suggests. The film's narrative is based on a series of journeys in which his prejudices are examined, and some are disposed of.

Robinson's interest in manufacturing, however, is rooted in his quasi-Surrealist practice. Whereas *London* set out to transform appearances through a more or less radical subjectivity, *Robinson in Space* addresses the production of actual space: the manufacture of artefacts and the development of sites, the physical production of the visible. Both films attempt to change reality with a heightened awareness in which 'I can always see how beautiful anything could be if only I could change it'[3] – the words of the Situationist text quoted in the opening sequence of *Robinson in Space* – but in the second, the initial interest is in the production of (at least some of) this *anything*. In the history of the modernist avant-gardes, the transformation of appearances by the poetic imagination preceded the design and construction of *new things*, and the identification of modernity was the bridge between the two. In a letter from Ethiopia, Rimbaud imagined a son who would become 'a famous engineer, a man rich and powerful through science'.[4]

An early motive for making the film was a curiosity about how imports of cars, electronics and other consumer goods reached the shops (apart from the cars, one hardly ever sees them in transit), and what, if any, were the exports that paid for them; so there is a lot of material dealing with ports.

In the Department of Transport's 1994 edition of *Port Statistics*,[5] based on figures for the twelve months of 1993, the Mersey Docks and Harbour Company was the most profitable port authority listed. Associated British Ports, which was not listed, declared a higher profit for 1993, but it operates twenty-two ports in the UK, including Southampton, Immingham and Hull. The MDHC bought the profitable Medway Ports in October 1993, and operates a ferry service and a container terminal in Northern Ireland, but it seems nonetheless that Liverpool was (and still is) 'the most profitable port in the UK'.

Reading these figures, I imagined there might be some exceptional reason for the MDHC's profitability – a one-off land sale, perhaps; commercial rents, or grant aid from the European Union. Like many people with a tourist's familiarity with the waterfronts of Liverpool and Birkenhead, I took the spectacular dereliction of the docks to be symptomatic of a past decline in their traffic, and Liverpool's impoverishment to be a result of this decline in its importance as a port. In fact, in September 1995, when the images of Liverpool in the film were photographed, Liverpool's port traffic was greater than at any time in its history.

In modern terms, individual British ports are not very large: Rotterdam – the world's biggest port – has an annual traffic of about 300 million tonnes. The UK has a long coastline and its traffic, though greater than ever, is divided among many ports. Since 1960, the tonnage of exports has quadrupled, increasing most rapidly in the 1970s, when North Sea Oil was first exploited. The tonnage of imports has fluctuated, and has risen overall by more than 20 per cent.

London is still the largest port in the UK (sixth-largest in the EU),[6] with a total of about 52 million tonnes in 1994. 'London', however, consists of the Port of London Authority's entire jurisdiction from Teddington Lock to Foulness – more than seventy miles of the Thames estuary. The largest single location of port activity is at Tilbury, where the docks are now owned by Forth Ports, but Tilbury itself is not a large port. Much of the traffic in the Thames is to and from other UK ports, especially that in oil. The total in *foreign* traffic for London and the Medway (which is a separate entity) is exceeded by the combined total for the Humber ports of Grimsby and Immingham, Hull, and the rivers Trent and Humber.

The second-largest total tonnage in 1994 was in the Forth estuary – 44 million tonnes, 68 per cent more than in 1993 – which is as fragmented as the Thames, and where the traffic is mostly oil. Next are the port authorities of Tees and Hartlepool, and Grimsby and Immingham, each with about 43 million tonnes. In these pairs, the Tees greatly exceeds Hartlepool and Immingham exceeds Grimsby, though to a lesser extent: Grimsby handles imports from Volkswagen and exports from Toyota. The traffic in the Tees estuary is largely bulk – imports of iron ore and coal for the steelworks at Redcar, exports of chemicals from the plants at Billingham and Wilton, and oil and petroleum products. A large figure for oil exports arises from the re-export of the product of a Norwegian field in the North Sea, which comes ashore by pipeline. There is not much container or semi-bulk traffic (timber, for example). The traffic at Immingham is also largely bulk – imports of iron ore and coal (3 million tonnes a year, the equivalent of 10 per cent of all the UK's deep-mined coal), imports of oil for the Immingham refineries, and chemicals into and out of quayside plants – KNAUF has an automated plasterboard plant at Immingham. In addition, there is some container and conventional traffic, and BMW, Volvo and Saab import cars.

The fifth- and sixth-largest tonnages are at Sullum Voe, an oil terminal in the Shetlands, with 39 million tonnes, almost entirely outgoing crude oil, and Milford Haven, with 34 million tonnes, again almost all oil. Southampton and Liverpool each handle about 30 million tonnes. Both have large container terminals – Liverpool has a large traffic in animal feeds, a new terminal for Powergen's coal imports and most of the UK's scrap metal exports. Southampton has a vehicle terminal – Renault, Rover, General Motors, Jaguar – and considerable oil imports.

The other two big ports in the UK are Felixstowe, which has the second-largest *non-oil* traffic (after London) and handles 40 per cent of *all* the UK's container traffic (50 per cent of its *deep-sea* container traffic), and Dover which, despite the Channel Tunnel, still handles 50 per cent of international roll-on-roll-off traffic (i.e. road goods vehicles) which in the last twenty years has become such a large part of international freight.

It is presumably a mistake to assess a port's importance solely by the tonnage of its traffic – a tonne of Colombian coal is worth about £28 at the destination port; a tonne of Volkswagens, say, £12,000; a tonne of laptop computers probably not less than £250,000. Container and road vehicle loads probably always represent considerably greater monetary value than bulk materials. On this basis, Felixstowe probably handles the traffic with the greatest value. However, given that other large ports are either fragmented (London), aggregates of two or more sites (Tees and Hartlepool, Grimsby and Immingham), or specialist in particular types of traffic (Sullum Voe is *all* oil exports, Felixstowe is *only* containers, Immingham and the Tees largely bulk), Liverpool can now be described as 'the UK's largest conventional port'. If Liverpool's relative importance is not what it was a hundred years ago, it is not because its traffic has declined, but because there is now much more port traffic, and there are more big ports.

Certainly, Liverpool's traffic did decline. In the early 1980s, it was down to about 10 million tonnes per year, but it is now about the same as it was in the mid 1960s. What has vanished is not the working port itself, even though most of the waterfront is derelict, but the contribution that the port made to the economy of Liverpool. Of all the United Kingdom's maritime cities, only Hull, which is much smaller, was as dependent on its port for wealth. Liverpool's population in 1994 was estimated at 474,000, just 60 per cent of the 789,000 in 1951. At its peak, the port employed 25,000 dock workers. The MDHC now employs about 500 dockers (and sacked 329 of these in September 1995). Similarly, a very large proportion of the dock traffic is now in containers and bulk, both of which are highly mechanised and pass through Liverpool without generating many ancillary jobs locally. The Channel Tunnel enables the MDHC to market Liverpool as a continental European port for transatlantic traffic, so that the ancillary jobs it supports may even be outside the UK. Also, like any English city outside London, Liverpool is now largely a branch-office location, and long ago lost the

Berkley Street, Liverpool 8, from *Robinson in Space* (1997)

headquarters establishments (White Star, Cunard) that made it a world city – the point of departure for emigrants from all over Europe to the New World.

Another influence on Liverpool's economy and culture has been the virtual elimination of the UK's merchant shipping fleet. According to Tony Lane, of Liverpool University's Sociology Department, although there were never more than about 250,000 seafarers in the British merchant fleet (about a third of whom were of Afro-Caribbean or Asian descent), seafarers were once the third most numerous group of workers in Liverpool.[7] The typical length of a seafarer's career was about seven years, so that a very high proportion of men in Liverpool had at some time been away to sea. Most of the few remaining British seafarers work on car, passenger or freight ferries, on which the majority of jobs are in catering. Apart from the decline in UK-owned ships and UK crews, modern merchant ships are very large and very sparsely crewed: there are never many ships in even a large modern port; they don't stay long, and crews have little – if any – time ashore, even assuming they might have money to spend. The P&O's *Colombo Bay*, for example, a large UK-registered container vessel, has a crew of twenty and a capacity of about 4,200 teu (twenty-foot-equivalent units) typically a mixture of twenty-foot and forty-foot containers, *each one of which* is potentially the full load of an articulated lorry. Presumably, jobs lost in port cities and on ships have to some extent been made up by expansion in the numbers of truck drivers.

Not only do ports and shipping now employ very few people, but they also occupy surprisingly little space. Felixstowe is the fourth-largest container port in Europe, but it does not cover a very large area. The dereliction of the Liverpool waterfront is a result not of the port's disappearance, but of its new insubstantiality. The warehouses that used to line both sides of the river have been superseded by a fragmented, mobile space: goods vehicles moving or parked on the UK's roads – the road system as a publicly funded warehouse. This is most obvious on summer evenings, when busy trunk roads on which parking is permitted become truck dormitories: south of Derby, an eighteen-mile stretch of the

A42, lined with lay-bys, that connects the M42 with the M1 is one of these, the nine-mile stretch of the A34 between Oxford and the M40 another. Many of these trucks are bound for the enormous warehouses of inland distribution estates near motorway junctions – Wakefield 41, for example, at junction 41 of the M1, next to its junction with the M62. The road haulage – or *logistics* – industry does not typically base its depots in port cities, though it is intimately linked to them: the road construction battlefields of Twyford Down and Newbury were the last obstacles to rapid road access to the port of Southampton from London (by the M3) and from the Midlands and the North (by the M40 to the A34). The relative insubstantiality of industrial development in the modern landscape seems to be accompanied by very high levels of energy consumption.

Despite having shed the majority of its dockers, the Liverpool port employer's attitude to its remaining workforce is extremely aggressive. In September 1995, two weeks after telling *Lloyd's List* that it had the most productive workforce in Europe,[8] the MDHC sacked 329 of its 500 remaining dockers after they refused to cross a picket line. Five employees of a contract labour firm had been sacked in a dispute over payment periods for overtime, and this led to the picket line that the MDHC workers refused to cross. Liverpool dockers were supported by secondary actions in New York and elsewhere, so that the giant US container line ACL threatened to move its ships from Liverpool unless the lockout was ended. In other countries, even employers were shocked by the MDHC's unrestrained determination to be rid of most of their last few dockers. In July 1996, ACL carried out their threat and moved their ships to Thamesport, an independently owned container terminal within the MDHC-owned Medway Ports in Kent (ACL later returned to Liverpool). Medway Ports, which had been privatised in 1989 as a management-employee buyout, was bought by the MDHC in 1993 in a transaction that made Medway's former chief executive a multi-millionaire. Medway had previously sacked 300 of *its* dockers for refusing to accept new contracts. On dismissal,

Sheerness, from *Robinson in Space* (1997)

the dockers were obliged to surrender their shares in the company at a valuation of £2.50 per share, shortly before MDHC bought them for £37.25 each.

The main port of the Medway is Sheerness, which is the largest vehicle-handling port in the UK, with imports by Volkswagen-Audi, two-way traffic by Peugeot-Citroën and exports from General Motors' UK plants, among others. Like other modern UK ports, it is a somewhat *out-of-the-way* place. Opposite the dock gates is the plant of Co-Steel Sheerness, which recycles scrap into steel rod and bar. Co-Steel, a Canadian company, is the protagonist of what it calls 'total team culture', in which all employees are salaried, overtime is unpaid, and union members fear identification. In June 1996, the International Labour Organisation called on the UK government to investigate Co-Steel's anti-union practices. On the other side of the Isle of Sheppey, at Ridham Dock (a 'hitherto little-known port' which featured in the Scott enquiry,[9] from which Royal Ordnance military explosives were shipped to Iran), there is another KNAUF automated plasterboard plant, which the 1995 Medway Ports' *Handbook and Directory* describes as 'the fastest running production line in Europe'. Opposite Sheerness, on the end of the Isle of Grain, is the automated container terminal of Thamesport, to which ACL's ships were diverted from Liverpool. In the Medway Ports' *Handbook*, Thamesport is described as the UK's most sophisticated container terminal, 'where driverless computerised cranes move boxes around a regimented stacking area with precision and speed'. Thamesport's managing director insists nonetheless: 'This is a people industry. The calibre and commitment of people is absolutely critical.' When Thamesport recruited its 200 staff, 'I did not want anyone with experience of ports because this is not a port – it's an automated warehouse that just happens not to have a lid on it.'

In England, only 1.1 per cent of employees work in agriculture, but the UK grows far more food than it did a hundred years ago, when the agricultural workforce was still large. In 1995, unemployment in Liverpool was 14 per cent. On Teesside, which is arguably 'the UK's biggest *single* port', are British Steel's plant at Redcar, and Wilton, the huge chemical plant now shared by ICI with Union Carbide, BASF, and DuPont. British Steel is now the world's third-largest steel producer, with substantial exports, and the chemical industry is one of the UK's most successful, with an export surplus of £4 billion. Nearby is the new Samsung plant at Wynyard Park. Despite this concentration of successful manufacturing industry and the port, unemployment in Middlesborough, on Teesside, is 17 per cent: the highest in the country. Wages in some parts of the UK are apparently now lower than in South Korea.

In the 1980s there were attempts to assert that the future of the UK's economy lay in services, and that the imbalance in imports of manufactured goods that characterised the Thatcher years could be sustained through increased exports of services (particularly 'financial services'). In fact, because of the virtual disappearance of the merchant shipping fleet, the service sector's share of exports has actually declined since 1960, and imports of cars, electronics and other *visible* items (there are few toys, for instance, not now marked 'made in China') are balanced by exports not of services but of other manufactured items, in particular intermediate products (for example, chemicals) and capital goods (power stations, airports). These strengths seem to match the financial sector's cultural preferences: chemical plants are capital-intensive, but do not involve the risks and ephemerality of product design; exports of capital goods are, by definition, financed by other people's capital. The UK is good at low-investment, craft-based high technology, but not at high-investment mass-production high technology, unless it is owned and financed elsewhere (the United States, Japan, South Korea or Germany). The UK's most extensive indigenous high-technology industry is weaponry, in which investment is supported by the state. It appears that the decline in manufacturing industry that has been so widely lamented, typically by design-conscious pro-Europeans who grew up in the 1960s (like myself), has been a partial phenomenon.

The UK's production of *desirable* artefacts is certainly lamentable (and confirms the stereotype of a nation run by Philistines with unattractive attitudes to sexuality), but any perception of the demise of manufacturing industry based on its failure to produce technologically sophisticated, attractive consumer goods is bound to be overstated. Most UK manufacturing is unglamorous – intermediate products and capital goods are not branded items visible in the shops. Intermediate products, in particular, are often produced in out-of-the-way places like Sheerness or Immingham – places at the ends of roads. The UK's domestically owned manufacturing sector is now small, but its most successful concerns are efficient, highly automated, and employ only a few people, many of whom are highly specialised technicians. The UK's *foreign-owned* manufacturing sector employs larger numbers of people in the production of cars, electronic products or components and other visible, but internationally branded, items: many General Motors cars built in the UK are badged as Opels, Ford now produces Mazdas (Ford owns 25 per cent of Mazda) at Dagenham, and the UK now has export surpluses in televisions and computers. The big export earners in manufacturing, like the ports, have a tendency to be invisible.

The juxtaposition of successful industry and urban decay in the UK's landscape is certainly not confined to the north of the country. A town like Reading, with some of the fastest growth in the country (Microsoft, US Robotics, Digital, British Gas, Prudential Assurance) offers, albeit to a lesser degree, exactly the same contrasts between corporate wealth and urban deprivation: the UK does not look anything like as wealthy as it really is. The dilapidated *appearance* of the visible landscape, especially the urban landscape, masks its prosperity. It has been argued that in eighteen years of Conservative government the UK has slipped in a ranking of the world's most prosperous economies in terms of Gross Domestic Product (GDP) per head, but it is equally likely that the position has remained unchanged, and in any case this is a ranking among nations all of which are becoming increasingly wealthy. If the UK has slipped in this table, it has not slipped anything like as much as, say, Australia or Sweden, or even the Netherlands. The UK's GDP is the fifth-largest in the world, after the United States, Japan, Germany and France. What has changed is the distribution of wealth.

In the UK, wealth is not confined to a Conservative *nomenklatura*, but the condition of, say, public transport or state-sector secondary schools indicates that the governing class does not have a great deal of use for them. People whose everyday experience is of decayed surroundings, pollution, cash-starved public services, job insecurity, part-time employment or freelancing tend to forget about the UK's wealth. We have been inclined to think that we are living at a time of economic decline, to regret the loss of the visible manufacturing economy, and to lower our expectations. We dismiss the government's claims that the UK is 'the most successful enterprise economy in Europe', but are more inclined to accept that there might be less money for schools and hospitals, if only because of the cost of financing mass unemployment.

There is something Orwellian about this effect of dilapidated everyday surroundings, especially when it is juxtaposed with the possibility of immediate virtual or imminent actual presence elsewhere, through telecommunications and cheap travel. Gradually, one comes to see dilapidation not only as an indication of poverty but also as damage inflicted by the increased centralisation of media and political control in the last two decades.

In the rural landscape, meanwhile, the built structures, at least, are more obviously modern, but the atmosphere is disconcerting. The windowless sheds of the logistics industry, recent and continuing road construction, spiky mobile phone aerials, a proliferation of new fencing of various types, security guards, police helicopters and cameras, new prisons, agribusiness (BSE, genetic engineering, organophosphates, declining wildlife), UK and US military bases (microwaves, radioactivity), mysterious research and training centres, 'independent' schools, eerie commuter villages, rural poverty, and the country houses of rich and powerful men of unrestrained habits are visible features of a landscape in which the suggestion of *cruelty* is never very far away.

In their book *Too Close to Call*, Sarah Hogg and Jonathan Hill describe the strategy behind the 1992 Conservative election campaign:

> Throughout the summer [1991], Saatchi's had been refining their thinking. Maurice Saatchi's thesis went like this. In retrospect at least, 1979, 1983 and 1987 appeared to be very simple elections to win. The choice was clear: 'efficient but cruel' Tories versus 'caring but incompetent' Labour. The difficulty for the Conservatives in 1991 was that the recession had killed the 'efficient' tag – leaving only the 'cruel'. While the Tory party had successfully blunted the 'cruel' image by replacing Margaret Thatcher with someone seen as more 'caring', Maurice did not believe that John Major should fight the election on soft 'caring' issues.[10]

In the subsequent period the Conservatives were seen as even less efficient and even more cruel. The shackling of women prisoners during labour, and its defence by Ann Widdecombe, the Home Office minister, was the most outrageous example of this, but the campaign to legitimise child-beating was perhaps more shocking because it was so widespread. The sexuality of Conservatism is certainly very strange. While there are always a few straightforward libertines among prominent Tories, and Thatcher apparently tolerated homosexuals when it suited her, repression and S&M haunt the Conservatives in a way that cannot be put down simply to the influence of the public schools. Like repression, deregulation inflicts pain and suffering. Unemployment, increased inequality, low wages and longer working hours all lead to depression, ill health and shorter life expectancy. In May 1996 Maurice Saatchi launched another pre-election campaign with the slogan: 'Yes it hurt. Yes it worked.'

This gothic notion evokes the famous passage in Burke's *Philosophical Inquiry*: 'Whatever is fitted in any sort to excite the ideas of pain, and danger, that is to say, whatever is in any sort terrible . . . is a source of the *sublime*.'[11] Alistair, Lord McAlpine of West Green, the Thatcher confidant who was party treasurer during her leadership, lived for most of these years as a tenant of the National Trust at West Green House in Hampshire. The house, which was badly damaged by fire during McAlpine's tenancy, and was bombed by the IRA after he had left, was built for General Henry 'Hangman' Hawley, who commanded the cavalry at Culloden; and over the door in the facade facing the garden is the inscription 'Fay ce que vouldras' ('Do what you will'), the quotation from Rabelais which was the motto of the Hell Fire Club.[12]

It takes a long time for a political and economic regime to change the character of a landscape. As I write in the last months of 1996, the regime is changing: in May 1996 Stephen S. Roach, chief economist at Morgan Stanley and former chief forecaster for the US Federal Reserve, announced that the doctrine of cost-cutting and real wage compression ('downsizing') of which he had been the most influential proponent for more than a decade, was wrong.[13] Companies would now have to hire more workers, pay them better and treat them better. In the UK, despite recovery in the housing market, whether or not Labour wins the forthcoming election, the attitudes of most leading UK companies to European social legislation and the single currency seem certain to eclipse the Tory right. The first services through the Channel Tunnel after the fire in November 1996 were international freight trains, the second of which was carrying car components from one Ford plant in the UK to another in Spain. The UK really is now (almost) a part of mainland Europe.

With the Conservatives and their obsessions removed, the new industrial landscape of the UK begins to resemble the computerised, automated, leisured future predicted in the 1960s. Instead of leisure, we have unemployment, a lot of low-paid service sector jobs, and a large number of people who are 'economically inactive', including 'voluntary' carers and people who have been *downsized* into a more or less comfortable early retirement, many of whom once worked for privatised utilities. The enormous irony of the Tory twilight is that their protestations that the UK is a prosperous *country* are largely true. There are even a few signs of a revival in the manufacture of indigenously financed high-technology consumer goods. The United Kingdom is a rich country in which live a large number of poor people and a similar number of reasonably well-off people who *say* they are willing to pay for renewal of the public realm. There *seems* to be no reason why the UK cannot afford a minimum wage, increased expenditure on welfare and education, incentives for industrial investment, environmental improvements, re-empowered local government, and other attributes of a progressive industrial democracy.

4

The Dilapidated Dwelling

Where I live, there seem to be two kinds of space. There is *new space*, in which none of the buildings are more than about ten years old, and there is *old space*, in which most of the buildings are at least twenty years old, a lot of them over ninety years old, and all are more or less dilapidated. Most of the *old space* is residential, but there are also small shops, banks, cafés, public houses, a health centre, a library, a social security office, schools, and so on. Most of the *new space* is occupied by large corporations of one sort or another, a few of them international in scope, and it is not urban in the conventional sense. It includes retail sheds; supermarkets; fast food restaurants; a Travel Inn; a business park; distribution warehouses; tyre, exhaust and windscreen service centres, and so on. Most of these places have large car parks and security cameras. There is a lot of new space under construction, it goes up fast, and more is proposed. Buildings in *new space* do not have to last very long. In some of the older *new space* the original buildings have already been replaced by new ones.

The *old space* looks poor, even when it isn't. Much of it is poor, but when it isn't, the dilapidation is still striking. *Old space* appears to be difficult to maintain. A lot of the shops don't look as if they're doing very well. The cybercafé didn't last very long. The public institutions, if they are lucky, manage to maintain their buildings. The public lavatories are in a terrible state, though they are very photogenic. In the street, there is a fair amount of outdoor drinking, and according to the police who attend burglaries, there is a lot of heroin about. A lot of houses have burglar alarms. Some have cable television or internet access.

At the moment, the residential property market is busy. There are always a lot of builders working, but most of them don't have the skills, the materials or the time to be particularly conscientious about anything beyond short-term performance. The conservationist is, as always, frustrated, and if anyone is responsible for the surfaces of *old space*, it is these builders and their clients.

In *old space*, apart from the smaller branches of banks and supermarket chains, the activities of large corporations are not very visible. A local estate agent, for example, is likely to be a major bank, building society or insurance company in disguise. Dilapidated houses are bought with mortgages from building societies, banks and other large corporations. A lot of small shops are franchises. The utility companies' installations are mostly underground, or in anonymous boxes which one tends not to notice. TV aerials and satellite dishes quickly blend with the domestic scene.

The dilapidation of *old space* seems to have increased, in an Orwellian way, with the centralisation of media and political power – by the disempowerment of local government, for instance. At the same time, experience of dilapidation is tempered by the promise of immediate virtual or imminent actual presence elsewhere, through telecommunications and cheap travel. As I stand at the bus stop with my carrier bags in the rain, I can window shop cheap tickets to Bali, or contemplate Hong Kong, Antarctica or Santa Cruz as webcam images on my Nokia; or I could if I had one – the virtual elsewhere seems, if anything, most effective as mere possibility, as a frisson.

New space is mostly work space. An increasing proportion of 'economically active' people work in *new space*. Most of those who are not 'economically active' visit it fairly frequently, at least for the weekly shop, but they do not spend much time there. A very large number of people are not 'economically active' – they are physically or mentally ill, children, non-working parents, 'voluntary' carers, the unemployed, pop stars in waiting, unpublished novelists, the early or otherwise retired, and other non-employed people. For these people, everyday surroundings are *old space*, and *old space* is mostly residential space – houses and flats. Residential space has a visiting workforce: the window cleaner, the decorator, the meter reader, the washing-machine engineer, the plumber, the small builder; and on-site earners – slaving away at Christmas crackers, clothes, poetry or television research. Despite the talk about corporate home-working and the long-expected 'death of the office', most of the above are likely to be self-employed, and very few of them at all well paid. The real economic activity of residential space – housework, most of it involved with child-rearing – is not paid at all. It was recently estimated that the real value of housework in the UK is £739 billion, 22 per cent more than the current value of the UK's GDP.[1] On average, people in the UK spend only 12 per cent of their total time in paid work.[2] Although unpaid, child-rearing is presumably the most significant of all economic activities in that it shapes – though not always directly – the values and attitudes of the next generation of wealth-creators. *New space*, on the other hand, is mostly corporate, company-car territory. There are plenty of women working in *new space*, often in senior roles, but the structures and work patterns in these places do not easily accommodate active parenthood. Most flexible part-time work suited to the child-rearer pays under £4 an hour.

In the UK, housing takes up around 70 per cent of urban land.[3] Its housing stock is the oldest in Europe, with an average age estimated at about sixty years. A quarter of the stock was built before the end of the First World War.[4] There are about 24 million dwellings in all,[5] but in the last twenty years the rate of new house-building has fallen to only 150,000 per year, largely because of the elimination of public-sector house-building.[6] In the UK, most new housing is built by developers for sale on completion, and is widely criticised as unsophisticated and overpriced.[7] In other developed economies, house production occurs in different ways, but if the UK is taken as the extreme example of a laissez-faire system operating in a built-up landscape with a restricted land supply, one can perhaps discern a general tendency, in that under advanced capitalism it is increasingly difficult to produce and maintain the dwelling. This is especially odd given that dwellings constitute the greater part of the built environment, that they are the spaces where most people spend most of their time, and where what is arguably the real 'work' of society is done. Modernity, it seems, is exemplified not so much by the business park or the airport, but by the dilapidated dwelling.

During the last twenty years or so, domestic life has been transformed in many more or less electronic ways: supermarket distribution, increased unemployment and early retirement, programmable gas heating, computerised banking, new TV, video, audio, telecommunications, the personal computer and the internet. Most of these things make it easier to stay at home, and many of them make it more difficult to go out, but the house itself has changed very little. The supermarkets, with computerised distribution and warehousing, and big trucks on modern roads, have transformed the UK's food market and shopping habits, creating a mass market in cosmopolitan food and drink that was previously only available in a few parts of London. In the same period, house production has merely declined, though supermarkets now offer mortgages. For the corporate economy, the house seems to exist only as a given, a destination for sales of consumable materials and services.

There are many reasons why this might be the case. Firstly, houses last a long time. House-building is also by its nature a very local undertaking, even for the largest producers. Wimpey, which claims to be the largest house-builder in the world, only seems to advertise its developments locally. The tendencies in production that have brought Ford to the Mondeo – the world car – have never been widely applied to house production. Despite the best efforts of several generations of architects, houses are still not manufactured off-site, and are not generally susceptible to *distribution*. When they are available in this way, the purchaser is faced with the problem of finding a site on which to erect a single house, which in the UK is very difficult. IKEA have started to produce prefabricated dwellings, but so far for assembly by the company itself only on its own development sites. There have been many impressive examples of factory-produced houses since the eighteenth century, but never in very large numbers.

In the middle of the nineteenth century, less than 1 per cent of the UK's national income was spent on house-building.[8] Since before the time of Engels, industrial capitalism has been more typically accompanied by the production of large but insufficient numbers of poor-quality houses, palatial workplaces, and a small number of millionaires' mansions: the Rothschilds' houses of Mentmore and Waddesdon, for example, or Bill Gates's $50 million house on the shores of Lake Washington, near Seattle. It seems that, for capitalism, houses are a means of centralising wealth, rather than products to be distributed. In the last hundred years, relative to earnings, food and most manufactured goods have become much cheaper, but houses have become more expensive both to build and to buy. Industrial production has not been very successful at producing houses for the people who are otherwise its consumers: most of the best housing developments of the last century or so seem to have been undertaken outside the market, by philanthropic employers, civic bodies or committed individuals and groups.

Since the late 1970s, 'housing' has been an unfashionable subject for architects and theorists. With a few notable exceptions – the architecture of Walter Segal, for instance – there has been very little house-building of any architectural interest in the UK beyond a few one-off houses, these often for architects themselves. Among theorists and other writers, the very idea of *dwelling* has been recognised as problematic. For example:

Architects have long been attacking the idea that architecture should be essentially stable, material and anchored to a particular location in space. One of the main targets for those who would make architecture more dynamic is of course that bulwark of inertia and confinement, the outer casing of our dwelling place that we call a house. Which explains why, as early as 1914, the Futurists put their main emphasis – at least in theory – on the complex places of transit:

'We are [the men] of big hotels, railway stations, immense roads, colossal ports, covered markets, brilliantly lit galleries . . .'

. . . We are dissatisfied because we are no longer able to come up with a truly promising form of architecture in which we would like to live. We have become nomads, restlessly wandering about, even if we are sedentary and our wanderings consist of flipping through the television channels.[9]

On the other hand:

Bridges and hangars, stadiums and power stations are buildings but not dwellings; railway stations and highways, dams and market halls are built, but they are not dwelling places. Even so, these buildings are in the domain of our dwelling. That domain extends over these buildings and yet is not limited to the dwelling place.[10]

In a culture in which so much of the space of work and transit is new, modern and professionally produced, but so much home space is old, amateurish and artlessly hand-made, one tends to forget that, like the industrial landscapes that inspired the modernist avant-gardes, the corporate economy only exists because it has been able to develop global markets in the necessities and longings of domestic life.

The dominant narratives of modernity – as mobility and instant communication – appear to be about *work* and *travel*, not *home*. They are constructions of a work-oriented academic élite about a work-oriented business élite. However, as Saskia Sassen points out, 'a large share of the jobs involved in finance are lowly paid clerical and manual jobs, many held by women and immigrants':

The city concentrates diversity. Its spaces are inscribed with the dominant corporate culture but also with a multiplicity of other cultures and identities. The dominant culture can encompass only part of the city. And while corporate power inscribes non-corporate cultures and identities with 'otherness', thereby devaluing them, they are present everywhere. This presence is especially strong in our major cities which also have the largest concentrations of corporate power. We see here an interesting correspondence between great concentrations of corporate power and large concentrations of 'others'. It invites us to see that globalisation is not only constituted in terms of capital and the new international corporate culture (international finance, telecommunications, information flows) but also in terms of people and non-corporate cultures. There is a whole infrastructure of low-wage, non-professional jobs and activities that constitute a crucial part of the so-called corporate economy.[11]

Dwellings are rarely corporate space (see Billy Wilder's *The Apartment*). Are dwellings 'other'? The 'other' space in the city centres, where corporate power is concentrated, is usually the dwelling space of 'other' cultures and identities. The dwellings of corporate insiders are usually located at a distance, but even they live in homes that represent a level of investment per square metre that is only a fraction of that made in their workplaces. At the same time, domesticity is characterised by intimacy, the 'nearness' that Kenneth Frampton noted as increasingly absent from architecture,[12] presumably most of all from corporate architecture. Perhaps these qualities of domesticity are 'other' to the corporate economy, even in the homes of corporate insiders? Perhaps we are all 'others' when we are at home?

> Marginality is today no longer limited to minority groups, but is rather massive and pervasive; this cultural activity of the non-producers of culture, an activity that is unsigned, unreadable and unsymbolised, remains the only one possible for all those who nevertheless buy and pay for the showy products through which a productivist economy articulates itself. Marginality is becoming universal. A marginal group has now become a silent majority.[13]

Heidegger's formulation of *dwelling* certainly sounds unfashionable:

> *Only if we are capable of dwelling, only then can we build.* Let us think for
> a while of a farmhouse in the Black Forest, which was built some
> two hundred years ago by the dwelling of peasants. Here the self-
> sufficiency of the power to let earth and heaven, divinities and
> mortals enter *in simple oneness* into things, ordered the house. It
> placed the farm on the wind-sheltered mountain slope looking
> south, among the meadows close to the spring. It gave it the wide
> overhanging shingle roof whose proper slope bears up under the
> burden of snow, and which, reaching deep down, shields the cham-
> bers against the storms of the long winter nights. It did not forget
> the altar corner behind the community table; it made room in its
> chamber for the hallowed places of childbed and the 'tree of the
> dead' – for that is what they call a coffin there: the *Totenbaum* – and
> in this way it designed for the different generations under one roof
> the character of their journey through time. A craft which, itself
> sprung from dwelling, still uses its tools and frames as things, built
> the farmhouse.[14]

This was the essay invoked by Kenneth Frampton towards the end
of his *Modern Architecture: A Critical History* as a recognition of a
quality of experience that many believed most modern building
had lost; this loss being, they said, why many people had rejected
modern architecture, and why, perhaps, we have speculative house-
builders who build houses for sale that are supposed to resemble
the tied cottages of Victorian farm workers.

Richard Sennett, in a lecture in 1992, pointed out that Heidegger
neglected the stupefying nature of *dwelling*, and that in fact *dwelling*
and *thinking* are antithetical. The creativity of cities, said Sennett,
arises from their being sites of unresolved conflict between *thinking*
and *dwelling*.

It is easy to poke fun at Heidegger's notion of dwelling – so
nostalgic, so conservative, so agricultural – so at odds with a
quasi-nomadic hunter-gatherer present as to be unhelpful, if not
actually undesirable, especially in the context of Heidegger's

involvement with Nazism in the 1930s. Although the house he evokes is exemplary as a work of architecture (and has the required longevity), the social fabric – the *dwelling* – that produced it is almost unattainable, unsupportable, though perhaps not quite. In a letter responding to some questions about house-building, a friend wrote:

> Recently we visited together with students of architecture the small village Halen in Switzerland, designed by Atelier 5, still located in an unspoiled forest. The extremely narrow terraced houses with small private courtyards and a central public place, built more than 30 years ago, were in a perfect state, well kept, partly modernised (insulation of the external walls). The common installations like the shop in the piazza, the petrol station, the swimming pool and the tennis lawn were still working and in good condition. The community, now living in the houses, were to a high percentage the children and grandchildren of the initial owners. They have returned after they first had left the houses of their parents.

Frampton has described Siedlung Halen as 'one of the most seminal pieces of land settlement built in Europe since the end of the Second World War . . . a model for reconciling development with place-creation and with the maintenance of ecological balance'.[15] If Halen represents something approaching the modern attainment of Heidegger's *dwelling*, as Frampton seems to suggest by his subsequent reference to Heidegger, it is intriguing to learn that many of those who live there occupy the houses of their parents.

We are more familiar with this kind of *dwelling* in the context of its loss. In a World Service radio interview, a Bosnian refugee in Mostar longs to return to his house in Stolac, fifty kilometres away, from which he was evicted by his Croat neighbours, even though the town is still under Croat control: 'My family has lived in Stolac for centuries . . . I love the smell of the river.' For most of us, there is another kind of *dwelling*.

The purpose of this work is to ... bring to light the models of action characteristic of users whose status as the dominated element in society (a status that does not mean that they are either passive or docile) is concealed by the euphemistic term 'consumers'.

... In our societies, as local stabilities break down, it is as if, no longer fixed by a circumscribed community, tactics wander out of orbit, making consumers into immigrants in a system too vast to be their own, too tightly woven for them to escape from it.

... Increasingly constrained, yet less and less concerned with these vast frameworks, the individual detaches himself from them without being able to escape them and can henceforth only try to outwit them, to pull tricks on them, to rediscover, within an electro-nicised and computerised megalopolis, the 'art' of the hunters and rural folk of earlier days.[16]

If we think of ourselves as *consumers* in this way, perhaps our difficulties with housing are easier to understand. How is housing *consumed?*

In the context of the urban home in the UK, de Certeau's notion of 'tactics' as a response to the predicament of being a consumer evokes not so much do-it-yourself – currently a bigger market in the UK than new house-building – but the way that the character of the public-sector housing 'estate' is changing 'as local stabilities break down'. In inner London and elsewhere, the system of allocating public-sector housing on a basis which reflected its philanthropic origins in the nineteenth century has been fractured since the 1970s by ideas like the 'hard-to-let' flat, by the 'right to buy' and by an increase in social mobility generally. Public-sector housing was financed by sixty-year loans, and was often designed by critically respected architects. It aimed to be of far better quality than that produced by the private sector. Often the more architecturally ambitious developments (including some influenced by the model of Halen) were difficult to build and were regarded as problematic early in their history, but some of them have aged well and have gradually accumulated populations who find them attractive as places to live.

Alexandra Road Estate, London NW8, in 1999, designed by Neave Brown of London Borough of Camden's Architects Department in 1968, completed in 1978

Whatever the wider implications, perhaps architects can take some comfort from this. The notion of 'the everyday' in architecture offers a welcome relief from conventional interpretations of architectural value, especially in a culture where most 'everyday' building is not produced with much architectural intention, but it seems to affirm the spatial quality and detail of architects' architecture where it exists. Similarly, the subjective transformations of spatial experience characteristic of both the Surrealists and the Situationists might seem to promise a way of transcending assumptions of spatial poverty, of transforming 'even the most colourless' localities, as Breton said of Aragon's 'spellbinding romantic inventiveness',[17] but in practice both groups were quite selective about the sites they favoured. In the long run, spatial and other architectural qualities seem to survive, though often not in the way that was expected.

The UK's new Labour government seems to be prepared to leave house-building to the private sector, even for the showcase Millennium Village development next to the dome at Greenwich. The long-term success of the Lansbury estate in Poplar, which was built as the housing showcase for the 1951 Festival of Britain, has not prompted Labour to recall that its commitment to public-sector housing produced so many internationally acclaimed housing developments between 1945 and the early 1970s. Not long before the 1997 election, Richard, Lord Rogers, newly ennobled in preparation for a Labour victory, presented an edition of the BBC's *Building Sights* – in which celebrities present favourite buildings – for which he selected the former London County Council's Alton Estate at Roehampton in south-west London – the Modern Movement landmark of 1952–59. This timely endorsement of the heroic period of public-sector housing seems not to have awakened any enthusiasms among members of the new government.

Instead, Labour has said little about housing, but appears to be giving tacit support to various private-sector proposals for 'supervillages': 5,200 new houses near Peterborough; 3,000 at Micheldever in Hampshire; between 5,000 and 10,000 houses west of Stevenage, and 3,300 houses in three new villages near Cambridge, 'masterplanned' by the architect Terry Farrell for a consortium of Alfred McAlpine, Bryant and Bovis in 'Cambridgeshire vernacular', an attempt to create 'a traditional village, with village greens with cricket pavilions, local shops and pubs' and a 69,677-square-metre business park. With or without cricket pavilions, none of these developments sound as if they will have much chance of either 'reconciling development with place-creation and the maintenance of ecological balance' or attempting to reconfigure the house as something approaching a successful industrial product.

Labour's belief in finding an accommodation with the market seems to preclude a revival of public-sector house-building on anything like its former scale, but the history of house-building suggests that the market will never be able to modernise *dwelling* on its own, and Labour is committed to modernisation. If there is to be any possibility for a more promising approach to *dwelling*, it is very unlikely to come from the conventional house-building industry. Some of the most successful house-building projects in the UK during the last two decades have been non-commercial initiatives that included houses for sale. In the Netherlands, the government's VINEX policy aims to build 800,000 dwellings by the year 2000, in a planned programme with commitments to credible architectural design and environmental and transport policies. This approach produces domestic architecture for sale of a quality that house buyers in the UK can only dream about. If house production in the UK is to undergo any kind of consumer-led reform, it looks as if this can only happen in the context of similar collectivist initiatives.

5

Popular Science

During the 1980s, I spent a lot of time looking out of a window of the third-floor flat in which I lived and worked in London. The window faced west towards Battersea Power Station, about three kilometres away. I lived in this flat for almost exactly ten years, during which the landscape that it overlooked changed in various ways. In 1983, the Central Electricity Generating Board (as it then was) ceased to operate Battersea, arguing that a relatively small power station in the middle of London was uneconomic. A competition was announced for commercial developers to propose new uses for the building and the surrounding site, which was large and extremely valuable. The winner was the owner of the most successful theme park in the UK who, with the explicit approval of the then prime minister, proposed to turn the structure into a theme park and invited her to return in two years' time to open it. Contractors gutted the building and removed the roof, installing two cranes which stuck out above the empty shell. The project then stalled amid suspicion that the long-term goal was to demolish the building and develop the site in more profitable ways. The developer sold the most successful theme park in the UK to raise funds to complete the project, but was unable to do so, and for some years the cranes remained on the site free to move in the wind – as they had to be so as not to be blown over. Sometimes they both faced one way, sometimes the other; sometimes they faced each other,

Battersea Power Station, London SW8, 1992

sometimes in opposite directions. Their movements were not that frequent, and didn't seem to be much connected with the weather, but gave the impression that the building was alive, and was perhaps thinking.

Inside the flat, we were thinking it would have been better if the power station had gone on working, or perhaps been replaced by a more modern one. In its day, Battersea Power Station was exemplary. Its exterior was designed by Sir Giles Gilbert Scott, a leading architect; its flue gases were 'scrubbed' clean; its city-centre position meant that energy lost in transmission was kept to a minimum, and its cooling water provided heating and hot water to a large number of dwellings on the opposite bank of the river. When it was closed, a boiler house had to be constructed to replace this function. Similar joint heat and power schemes are common in other countries. In England in the 1980s none of this counted for anything, but as a monument the building's future had to be guaranteed. The nearby Bankside Power Station opposite St Paul's Cathedral, also a work of Scott, has now been converted into the new Tate Gallery of Modern Art.

As we felt ourselves losing ground, both politically and economically, our sense of loss was partly mollified by observing these visible changes in the detail of the landscape, as spectators at some sporting event might watch the opposition winning. We might not like the way things were going, but at least we had a good view. Satellite dishes began to appear on the houses and flats visible from the window. We would notice them for the first time in the morning when they caught the sun, so that they seemed to have grown in the night. Soon we could see about twenty, then the rate of increase slowed. A couple of years later the dishes began to disappear. I began to think of the entire view as a very slow but visible movement of self-organising matter. Apollinaire's impression of the south London suburbs, seen from the train, was of 'wounds bleeding in the fog'. Sometimes it seemed possible to perceive the view as an organic phenomenon. There was a Kentucky Fried Chicken outlet nearby, so there was always plenty of animal protein lying about the streets. At other times, the perception was of molecular vibration, turbulence, consciousness even. From *The Importance of Being Earnest*, I recalled: 'Pray don't talk to me about the weather, Mr Worthing. Whenever people talk to me about the weather, I always feel quite certain that they mean something else.' In the narration of a film, I quoted Democritus: 'According to convention, there is a sweet and a bitter; a hot and a cold; and according to convention there is colour. In truth, there are atoms and a void.' Such abstraction leads to irony. I began to think it might be possible to predict the future by looking out of the window. In *The Anatomy of Melancholy* Robert Burton (who styled himself Democritus Junior, and is said to have accurately foretold the date of his own death) wrote: 'Democritus . . . was so far carried with this ironical passion, that the citizens of Abdera took him to be mad, and sent therefore ambassadors to Hippocrates the physician, that he would exercise his skill upon him.'[1] I decided to cure myself by making a film about London. Many details of the view from the window appeared in the film. Shortly before it was finished, we moved out of the flat.

In the summer of 1989, there were several bankruptcies among London property developers. The political atmosphere in the UK began to change. At first, this change seemed rather rapid, but it slowed. With the fall of the Berlin Wall, one vague unease was replaced by another. As we now know, on average, people in the DDR lived longer than Westerners – even wealthy Westerners – because they were more equal, and it is said that in the advanced economies more people now die as a result of depression than in car crashes. In a somewhat similar way, since pure science began taking a serious interest in the weather and other indeterminate, complex phenomena, the second law of thermodynamics has lost much of its melancholy allure, but phenomena like the fluctuations of the stock market have become part of 'nature'. Everything is 'nature'. Everything that exists in actuality, perhaps even every thought, dream or fantasy, must have some material basis or it wouldn't exist at all. Probably artists have always known this, but for many people it is distressing. How can human aberrations like nuclear power stations, neoliberal governments or uncomfortable clothing be 'natural' in the same way as wild flowers or thunder-storms? A spoilsport might assert that, though everything may be natural, not everything comes about in quite the same way; but that doesn't seem to diminish the sense of enlightenment.

In *Laughter* (1900), Henri Bergson wrote: 'Could reality come into direct contact with sense and consciousness, could we enter into immediate communion with things and with ourselves, probably art would be useless, or rather we should all be artists.'[2] About thirty years later, in Prague, in an essay 'What is Poetry?', Roman Jakobson wrote:

> Nowadays, the department-store mirror monstrosity and the village inn's tiny fly-bespattered pane of glass are considered to be of equal poetic worth. And just about anything can come flying out of them . . . No nook or cranny, no activity, landscape, or thought stands outside the pale of poetic subject matter.[3]

In the twentieth century, images of already-existing modern urban and industrial landscapes were involved in the production of new and influential buildings, and hence new landscapes: the photographs in Le Corbusier's *Vers une Architecture* (1923), those in László Moholy-Nagy's *Von Material zu Architektur* (1929), in Erich Mendelsohn's *Amerika* (1926). Though not realised, Archigram's proposals, similarly derived from observations of the already-existing, have diffused into much of the mainstream of international architecture in various ways, via the Pompidou Centre in Paris, for instance, or the Lloyd's building in London. OMA's buildings are accompanied by Rem Koolhaas's polemic of *bigness*, which is identified as a crucial characteristic of already-existing built environments beyond the conventional value systems of architectural criticism. In many of these modern examples, representational space – the image – and representations of space – the design – are the work of the same individual, or of practitioners of the same art form. Representational space – to use Lefebvre's term – and built environments are more usually produced by the practitioners of different art forms, and often at different times. For instance, the tradition of literary urbanism – if one can call it that – which includes De Quincey, Poe, Baudelaire, Rimbaud, Apollinaire, Aragon, Benjamin and Bataille – became highly influential in the architectural culture of the 1970s, so much so that many of these writers' texts are now required reading for shopping mall designers.

This division of labour is not surprising when one compares the work involved. Radical subjectivities tend to be inclusive, whereas design is ultimately a process of selection. Radical subjectivities in art, on the other hand, usually presuppose some outcome other than the artwork – 'a bridge between imagination and reality must be built' (Raoul Vaneigem, in *The Revolution of Everyday Life*), and 'to change life, however, we must first change space' (Henri Lefebvre, in *The Production of Space*). The *dérive* was not an end in itself – among the Situationists were architects: Constant's *New Babylon* was a physical proposal that offered a new built form for the society of *homo ludens*. In the UK recently there has been a remarkable revival of interest in the Situationist subjectivity of place, in psychogeography, but so far there has been little interest in the Situationists' architecture. *New Babylon* was based on an early recognition of the implications of information technology and automated production, which was to bring a freedom from work that has to some extent been realised, though not in quite the way it was envisaged. What has not been realised at all is any corresponding automation of the production of built structures. This has meant that in relative terms buildings have continued to become more expensive, while other goods have become cheaper. The volume of new construction is now less than it used to be, and western cities have not changed anything like as much as was expected in, say, the early 1960s. Most of the new landscapes which have evolved as a result of computer-driven change have been peripheral, and either ephemeral and relatively insubstantial – the logistics warehouse, the container port, the business park – or, if more substantial, have been realised only because they generate very high profits – the shopping mall, the airport. It is intriguing that some of the forms of these last two examples somewhat resemble those of Constant's unrealised architecture.

I am inclined to set the growing interest in the poeticisation of experience of landscapes – typically urban landscapes, but also those of railways, airports and various other industries, even agriculture – in an economic and political context. In the UK now there is a lot of official and other thinking about ways in which the anomalous high cost of built structures can be reduced. In the 1950s, for example, a new suburban house in the UK cost about as much as three new family cars. The price of a similar house in the 1990s would probably be about that of ten new cars. These cars will be more impressive products than the cars of the 1950s, and will last longer, whereas received opinion is that the houses of the 1990s are no better than those of the 1950s, and may well not last as long. This relative increase in the cost of buildings is evident in most 'advanced' economies, but is particularly marked in the UK, where the building industry is less mechanised and more deskilled, and the supply of land for building is highly constrained. Buildings and other infrastructure often seem surprisingly rudimentary or dilapidated to visitors from other industrialised countries, and in London especially, even relatively wealthy people often live in houses that are small, old and architecturally impoverished, but extraordinarily expensive.

In a context where building – not just the building of houses, but all building – has become more expensive, so that the volume of new construction is less than it used to be, new architecture has assumed a kind of scarcity value. It has become exotic, so that its representation and discussion in various media is now much more widespread than was the case when encounters with actual built architecture were more common. For most people, in most of the landscapes of 'advanced' economies, the transformation of every-day surroundings is achieved much less by physical rebuilding than by other means. Perhaps this is why an interest in the subjective transformation of landscape has become so widespread in recent years. In London now, psychogeography leads not so much to avant-garde architecture as to gentrification.

One wonders what to make of this. For government, the encouragement of gentrification, or some euphemism for it, seems to be a central strategy both for cities and in housing policy. The great irony of the UK's psychogeography phenomenon is that its invocation of the *flâneur* only narrowly preceded an almost immediate commodification of café culture. Downing Street advisors just back from Barcelona marvel at the sudden appearance of aluminium furniture on the pavements of northern cities. This phenomenon, and its residential counterpart, the 'loft', is now regarded as a principal means of urban regeneration. Lifestyle magazines discover the collectable qualities of Modern Movement public-sector housing developments, as flats in them begin to change hands on the open market. This notion of regeneration, where existing physical structures are socially reconstructed through acquisition and improvement, has been a familiar feature of life in London and other cities since the 1960s, when middle-class buyers 'discovered' run-down districts, usually in inner cities, and in doing so increased their value, rather in the way that the Surrealists 'discovered' the bric-a-brac of the flea market.

In the UK, the subjective transformation of landscape seems to offer the individual a way to oppose the poverty of everyday surroundings. As individuals, we can't rebuild the public transport system, or re-empower local democracy, but we can poeticise our relationship with their dilapidation. Perhaps this is a legacy of the 1980s when, in London at least, large parts of the city were visibly altered by a political force that was shocking, especially after the stagnation of the 1970s. Perhaps the impulse to poeticise landscape in this way always coincides with times of heightened political tension. In 1948, the Czech Surrealist Vratislav Effenberger made a film, *The Outline of a Study of a Fraction of Reality*, which survived only as a retrospectively created script, but apparently included images 'from the Prague loading dock and other deserted corners of the city'.[4] Effenberger's film was made in the same year as the Stalinist coup.

In 1974, in his introduction to *The Practice of Everyday Life*, Michel de Certeau identified the same predicament in a slightly different way:

> The purpose of this work is to . . . bring to light the models of action characteristic of users whose status as the dominated element in society (a status that does not mean that they are either passive or docile) is concealed by the euphemistic term 'consumers'.
>
> . . . Increasingly constrained, yet less and less concerned with these vast frameworks, the individual detaches himself from them without being able to escape them and can henceforth only try to outwit them, to pull tricks on them, to rediscover, within an electro-nicised and computerised megalopolis, the 'art' of the hunters and rural folk of earlier days.
>
> . . . Witold Gombrowicz, an acute visionary, gave this politics its hero . . . whose refrain is 'When one does not have what one wants, one must want what one has': 'I have had, you see, to resort more and more to very small, almost invisible pleasures, little extras . . . You've no idea how great one becomes with these little details, it's incredible how one grows.'[5]

Capitalism both destroys and creates places, but the places it creates seem always, at least to begin with, less substantial, less rich, than the places it destroys; as in the cases of, say, the mechanisation of agriculture and the ports, or the replacement of mining and other industries by landscapes of distribution and retailing. It is difficult to be certain, but judged simply by the numbers of people present, a modern port, for example, seems a reduced phenomenon compared with the seaports of earlier times. On the other hand, modern capitalism also gives place high value – partly by making its sought-after qualities scarce, partly by concentrating power in the global system in particular places: New York, Tokyo, Frankfurt, Paris, London, and so on. In the interstices of all this – in more or less dilapidated domestic spaces, as 'consumers' (neither passive nor docile) – we live our lives.

The Surrealists admired Gaudí, though Surrealism itself produced no architecture until the 1940s, in New York, when Frederick Kiesler aligned himself with the movement and developed a polemic for 'magic architecture', largely unbuilt but now influential. In a gesture which can be read in various ways, the Royal Institute of British Architects recently awarded its 1999 Royal Gold Medal to the city of Barcelona. A report of the award ceremony quoted Pasqual Maragall, former socialist mayor of Barcelona, comparing London under Thatcher with Barcelona under Franco: 'Cities have periods in history in which they do nothing because of their politicians', and 'the radical puritanism of Mrs Thatcher's government condemned the destitute to remain entrenched in their destitution'. Incapable of magic architecture, we made art out of our deprivation. I hadn't realised it was quite that bad. 'When one does not have what one wants, one must want what one has.'

6

Architectural Cinematography

Since its invention, the cinema has offered glimpses of what Henri Lefebvre described, in another context, as 'the preconditions of another life'.[1] As the most extensive way of reconstructing experience of the world, it was also the most extensive way of getting out of it, and into another one. It's not surprising that so much of cinema was created by, and to some extent for, people with first-hand experience of emigration.

The new, virtual world of cinema was typically a world transformed – by eroticism, love, solidarity, crime, war or some similarly extraordinary experience. It differed from that offered by, say, the novel in that it was visible, and in that usually the spaces of the new world were made by photographing fragments of the old one. These fragments were very often specially created for the purpose, but in practice it seems to make very little difference whether the *décor* of a film is real or artificial, or even whether a film is fiction or documentary. The newness of the spaces of the cinema is a product, not of set-building, but of cinematography. It's the phenomenon of *photogénie*.

The earliest reference that I know of to something like this is made in Louis Aragon's essay 'On *Décor*', which was first published in September 1918 in Louis Delluc's *Le Film*. This was Aragon's first published writing, in which he wrote:

To endow with a poetic value that which does not yet possess it, to wilfully restrict the field of vision so as to intensify expression:

these are two properties that help make cinematic *décor* the adequate setting of modern beauty.[2]

The first part of this statement – 'to endow with a poetic value that which does not yet possess it' – anticipates Aragon's identification of the Surrealist frisson in *Le Paysan de Paris* (1926), the 'new kind of novel' based on descriptions of two of the several places in Paris that the Surrealists had adopted:

> I felt the great power that certain places, certain sights exercised over me . . . The way I saw it, an object became transfigured: it took on neither the allegorical aspect nor the character of the symbol, it did not so much manifest an idea as constitute that very idea . . . I acquired the habit of constantly referring the whole matter to the judgement of a kind of frisson which guaranteed the soundness of this tricky operation.[3]

Later in the book, Aragon identifies a similar sensation as that which accompanies the recognition of a poetic image, and it has always seemed to me that, as a sensibility, the surrealist frisson very much resembles the momentary insight, the instant of identification of an image that sometimes results in a successful photograph, or an image in a film. One wonders, even, if it was partly Aragon's experience of the cinema that led him to the Surrealist subjectivity to actual everyday surroundings.

The second part of Aragon's statement – 'to wilfully restrict the field of vision so as to intensify expression' – effectively describes film space. Films are made of images with a field of view that is very narrow compared with experience of actual, three-dimensional space. The space of a film is assembled from fragments, their relationship inferred from cues in action, sound or narrative. Most film space is off-screen – either remembered from preceding images, or heard, or merely the imaginary extension of the space on screen. Because it is reconstructed in this way, film space is always a fiction, even when the film is a documentary.

In his book *Art of the Cinema* (1929), Lev Kuleshov describes making a sequence in *Engineer Prite's Project* (1917–18):

> It was necessary for our leading characters, a father and his daughter, to walk across a meadow and look at a pole from which electric cables were strung. Due to technical circumstances, we were not able to shoot all this at the same location. We had to shoot the pole at one location and separately shoot the father and daughter in another place. We shot them looking upward, talking about the pole and walking on. We intercut the shot of the pole, taken elsewhere, into the walk across the meadow.
>
> This was the most ordinary, the most childlike thing – something which is done now at every step.
>
> It became apparent that through montage it was possible to create a new earthly terrain that did not exist anywhere.[4]

Before I ever thought of making a film, I had developed a habit of identifying examples of what might be described as 'found' architecture, and documenting them with colour slides. Many were industrial structures of various kinds, including some of the types photographed by Bernd and Hilla Becher, whose work I knew a little. I had also come across the Surrealists' adoption of particular sites in Paris – the Tour Saint-Jacques, the Porte Saint-Denis, the abattoirs of La Villette, the Parc des Buttes-Chaumont, and so on – the last of which is one of Aragon's subjects in *Le Paysan de Paris*.

What began as a search for individual buildings gradually widened to include all sorts of details of everyday surroundings – odd ruined shopfronts, roofscapes, scaffolding, the spaces of the London underground, and so on. The subjectivity involved was very like that described by Aragon, or the state of mind that Walter Benjamin describes in his essays about Marseille. In the long run, the aim was to gradually refine the practice and transform even the most familiar spaces of the city centre – Piccadilly Circus, say, or Regent Street – but it was difficult to progress beyond a certain point without some technique in making images. I recovered the idea, almost inadvertently, in making a film about London over ten years later, by which time the process of defamiliarisation had become second nature.

By then I had made a number of short films, all of which were combinations of 16mm monochrome images of urban or rural landscapes and a fictional voice-over. To begin with, it had been difficult to see what one could make with sequences of architectural images, however intriguing, other than some kind of installation. To some extent, a sense of continuity could be achieved by making long takes with a moving camera (the first film was twenty minutes long, but contained only three shots) or by adopting the structure of a journey, but I had always thought that any film I might make would involve some kind of interior monologue. Ten years earlier, as an architecture student, I had seen Marker's *La Jetée* (1962).

The technique gradually evolved so that the films included more montage, with larger numbers of shorter shots. They were mostly made by undertaking journeys, but the pictures were rarely

Piancastagnaio, Province of Siena, Italy, from *The End* (1986)

planned, and were always subject to the unpredictability of natural light. The narration was always written after the footage had been shot and edited, so that the writing was determined by the picture, rather than the picture by the writing, and if one had put the pictures together in a different order, or shot different pictures, some other equally plausible fiction might be the result. It was very difficult to write coherent narration for an already-edited sequence of brief, spontaneous images, but it seemed a suitably modern, or even postmodern way to approach fiction. It also resembled the method of cinema newsreels. I found out later that other, more critically respected documentaries had been made in a similar way, without too many preconceptions. The combination of moving camera and interior monologue suggested some more-or-less comic attempt to represent consciousness, or perhaps artificial consciousness – the inner experience of an alienated and rather unreliable artificial *flâneur*. This was in homage both to *Frankenstein* and to the confessional voice-overs and subjective-camera sequences of *noir*.

The cinematography had also developed a distinct technique. Some of the best footage was shot directly following thunderstorms, or in windy weather at the coast. In this clear air, shadows were very sharp, detail was brightly illuminated, and the sky was darker, or at least not brighter, than the ground. It was possible to produce footage of unusual sharpness and richness of detail which achieved an almost three-dimensional quality, despite the limitations of 16mm. This seemed to confirm the preference for monochrome, and the old idea that the illusion of depth in photographs of architecture is often most convincing in fine-grain, high-contrast, deep-focus, monochrome pictures.[5]

On the other hand, this preference for particular kinds of daylight made it increasingly difficult to produce pictures. The various stylistic traits – interior monologues; the compressed writing of the voice-overs; the reliance on atmospheric effects – also encouraged allusions to genre: Gothic fiction, or even expressionism. The films were becoming stylised and increasingly

difficult to make. The quasi-Surrealism of the original project
seemed to have been diminished in the attainment of technique.

The previous three films had been made by going away from
London to more photogenic locations.[6] For various reasons, it
looked as if the time had come to make a longer film, which
suggested a more serious engagement with a subject. It also
suggested a longer period of cinematography, which would be
difficult if we had to go away. The political atmosphere of London
seemed to be changing, and it would be a challenge to try to
re-imagine familiar surroundings. I decided to risk attempting to
make a film about where I lived.

In the early 1990s, London did not seem a very promising
camera subject, especially for someone obsessed with clear air.
During the summer of 1989, when the film was conceived, visibility along the river was often so poor that one could stand on a
bridge and find it difficult to see the next one. On the other hand,
in the absence of traditional London fog, perhaps the traffic fumes
had possibilities. I wondered whether to make the film in colour,
which might be more suited to the haze.

It had occurred to me that if the film was to be longer than its
predecessors, it ought also to be wider. In any case, a feature-length
film for theatrical distribution would conventionally offer the more
extensive spectacle of 35mm cinematography, with the sharper
resolution that I sought for making architectural images. It was not
that much more expensive to shoot the film on 35mm stock. I was
worried that it would be very difficult to make monochrome images
of everyday surroundings in London – the film's documentary
aspect implied less freedom to abandon a subject if it proved too
difficult to get a decent shot out of it. Colour might not achieve the
vertiginous three-dimensionality of monochrome pictures, but it
would be much less dependent on the weather. I'd never liked the
look of most 16mm colour – for some reason, I didn't think it
would produce pictures that were sufficiently sharp or colour-satu-
rated, but this aversion to 16mm colour did not seem to apply to
35mm. Colour also seemed more likely to produce pictures that

were funny. Monochrome would have been too serious. For some time, I held on to the idea that some reels might be monochrome and some colour, like Warhol's *The Chelsea Girls*, but in the end, after testing various filmstocks, we decided to shoot the film on a 35mm, fine-grain, daylight colour stock that had recently been introduced by Eastman.

With colour, the camera became an instrument of criticism. A McDonald's, for instance, photographed in monochrome, might merely have looked a bit bleak; in colour it got a laugh. The slightest sense of hyperreality in the pictures seemed to be enough to unmask their subjects, especially if one stared at them a bit. I had already begun to use longer-focal-length lenses more often, with the result that the camera was hardly ever used without a tripod, and camera movement had become very infrequent. With colour, the camera hardly ever moved at all, the longer lenses were used even more, and the images were more often of details. This seemed to corroborate another idea one comes across in architectural photography, that colour suits images of detail.[7] It also recalled Aragon's formulation of *décor* – in re-imagining something as big as London, one tended to *restrict the field of vision*.

These characteristics, together with the adoption of rather stolid, often symmetrical compositions (easy to set up in a hurry), and the 4×3 screen ratio,[8] seemed to suit the spaces of London. There was an element of self-parody in the pictures, as if there was something inherently funny about their predictability. This quality was sometimes used to convey irony, affection and other meanings.

With the heavier 35mm equipment, and the frequent necessity to carry it some distance, each set-up was much more of a physical commitment than it had been before. This encouraged a tendency to linger, and make several shots, both with different lenses and of different details of the subject. Where there was a lot going on, it was possible to assemble action sequences, which created more extensive spaces than those of the earlier films. This was augmented by post-synchronised background sound which, laid over a group of shots, identified them as fragmentary views of the same location. None of this sound was ever recorded with the picture, and it was only rarely from the actual location. One of the sound effects in *London* had been recorded for *Blow-Up* over twenty-five years earlier. We chose this, without knowing what it was, because the level of background traffic roar was much lower than usual. One of the film's biggest fictions was that it reconstructed London as a quiet city, without the noise of traffic.

It was organised as the record of a period of about ten months. The off-screen narrator described the work of a fictitious character who was researching what he described as the 'problem' of London, which seemed to be, in essence, that it wasn't Paris. There was a document, a plan, with a large reserve of ideas for subjects and itineraries, but the film effectively made itself up as the events of the year (1992) unfolded.[9] It was mostly photographed by a crew of two. We went out with the camera regularly on two days in every week, and shot some other material at night or at weekends. Apart from coverage of particular events, the photography was nearly always determined on the day, or at fairly short notice. Altogether, there were about one hundred days of photography, and one hundred 400-foot rolls of film – about seven-and-a-half hours of material. We stopped when we thought we had enough material to make the film, which was about when we had expected. Most of the material in the film appears in the order it was shot. It was edited and written in more or less the same way as the earlier films, though there was more material and a lot of work post-synchronising sound, and for the first time I worked with an editor[10] – a collaboration that has survived this and subsequent projects.

Since *London*, two more films of about the same length have been made in more or less the same way,[11] though with tighter schedules and itineraries. In the latest film, there is more camera movement. This is not a satire, but an investigation of some aspects of housing in the UK, a documentary made for television. It was shot in digital video and includes interviews with academics and other specialists.

At the moment, it looks as if the future of this architectural cinema depends on developing ways to assemble more extensive and ambitious fictional spaces. *London* and its sequel *Robinson in*

Space set out to re-imagine actual spatial subjects. The latest film addresses the difficulty of making new spaces. The next project might explore the creation of a *new earthly terrain* like that of Kuleshov, a fictitious world made from fragments of the real one.

Film offers a kind of permanence to subjectivity. On a bad day, or in a bad light, even the architecture of Gaudí might lose its immediate appeal, but in a film, the transitory experience of some ordinary, everyday detail as breathtaking, euphoric or disturbing – a doorway, perhaps, or the angle between a fragment of brickwork and a pavement – can be registered on photographic emulsion and relived every time the material is viewed. On the other hand, when actual extra-ordinary architecture is depicted in films it's often easy to conclude that something is missing, as if the camera has nothing sufficiently revelatory to add, nothing to improve on a visit to the actual building.

At about the time I first began to think about making a film, I particularly admired the architecture of Hans Scharoun, on one hand, and *film noir*, on the other. Until recently, it never occurred to me to look for a connection between them, other than perhaps Berlin. Scharoun's Philharmonie, for example, and, say, Fritz Lang's films of the 1940s and '50s – *The Big Heat*, *Human Desire*, and so on – don't seem to have much in common until one remembers that both architect and film-maker share a background in the expressionism of the 1920s. Quite what, if anything, this might mean isn't clear, though it's intriguing that Scharoun's influence does seem to be present in the work of some present-day architects who attempt connections with the spatiality of film. The architecture of Scharoun and Hugo Häring might just be seen as confirming the rationality of the apparently eccentric (though I doubt that they saw it that way), whereas *noir* reveals the irrationality of the normal, so perhaps the two are in some way complementary. Certainly, both extra-ordinary experience of everyday architecture (in film, especially *film noir*) and everyday experience of extra-ordinary architecture (expressionism, Art Nouveau and so on), might be sought for similar reasons. The Surrealists, for instance, admired both Gaudí and *film noir*. For anyone in pursuit of, let's say, the *improvement* of everyday life, a medium which offers a heightened awareness of architecture – the medium of film – might be thought at least as compelling as an actually existing architecture of heightened awareness – an *ecstatic* architecture, whatever that might be.

7

London in the Early 1990s

In the autumn of 1989 I began to research an idea for a film about London, which was subsequently commissioned by the British Film Institute and photographed over a period of about ten months in 1992. The first print of the completed film, by then called *London*, was delivered in January 1994, just in time for that year's Berlin Film Festival. It was well received in Berlin, and was released in the UK the following June, where it played in a succession of West End cinemas for most of the summer. For a film like this – without a visible cast, or even much of a narrative – to be even a minor box office proposition was extremely unusual, and its relative success was probably at least partly due to the possibility it offered audiences of finding aspects of their everyday experience represented in the cinema. The film opened at the Institute of Contemporary Arts, in the Mall, and departing audiences walked out of the cinema into the space of one of its sequences (the rehearsal for Trooping the Colour), which had been photographed from the ICA's balcony. The film set out to document, among other things, the 'decline' of London under the Tories, and it offered people the morale-boosting opportunity to share thoughts that had perhaps previously occurred to them only in isolation. As a portrait of the city, it was rather critical – in those days, Londoners were proud, not so much of London, but of themselves for putting up with its physical and other shortcomings. One would not be permitted to say such things today.

One of the starting points for the film was a passage from the
memoirs of Alexander Herzen (1812–70):

> There is no town in the world which is more adapted for training one
> away from people and training one into solitude than London. The
> manner of life, the distances, the climate, the very multitude of the
> population in which personality vanishes, all this together with the
> absence of Continental diversions conduces to the same effect. One
> who knows how to live alone has nothing to fear from the tedium of
> London. The life here, like the air here, is bad for the weak, for the
> frail, for one who seeks a prop outside himself, for one who seeks
> welcome, sympathy, attention; the moral lungs here must be as strong
> as the physical lungs, whose task it is to separate oxygen from the
> smoky fog. The masses are saved by battling for their daily bread, the
> commercial classes by their absorption in heaping up wealth, and all
> by the bustle of business; but nervous and romantic temperaments,
> fond of living among people, fond of intellectual sloth and of idly
> luxuriating in emotion, are bored to death here and fall into despair.[1]

This passage is part of Herzen's account of the period soon after
his arrival in 1852, when London was physically very different from
the city it is now (much more so than it was by, say, 1900), but it was
easy to connect it with one's experience of London in the 1980s.
Other people said similar things – I recall, for instance, Zaha
Hadid's suggestion that London was a good place to work, because
there were so few distractions.

The film took the form of a fictional journal (like Daniel Defoe's
Journal of the Plague Year), an unnamed narrator's account of the project
of his companion and ex-lover Robinson, a disenfranchised, would-
be intellectual, petty bourgeois part-time lecturer at the 'University of
Barking'. Robinson's project was a study of 'the problem of London',
and the problem of London seemed to be, in essence, that it wasn't
Paris. I had read up on the experiences of various nineteenth-century
visitors from France, on the look out for further details of 'the
absence of Continental diversions', and discovered Paul Verlaine's
description of London as 'flat as a bed-bug, if bed-bugs were flat',

and his suggestion that the way people drank in pubs confirmed the 'lamentable inferiority of Anglo-Saxons'.[2] Apollinaire's description of the south London suburbs, seen from the train, was of 'wounds bleeding in the fog'. Wilhelm Kostrowicki, before he became Apollinaire, had visited London twice in pursuit of a young woman called Annie Playden, whose family lived in Landor Road, SW9, and who soon afterwards emigrated to Texas, where she was discovered by academics in 1951, unaware of her rejected suitor's subsequent identity.[3] Reading Enid Starkie's biography,[4] I found that Arthur Rimbaud probably produced a good deal of his literary output in London (there are likely images of London in, for example, the *Illuminations*), and that his last address in England was not in Scarborough, as had been suggested, but in Reading. This became the starting point for a sequel to *London, Robinson in Space* (1997), in which Robinson is exiled to the English provinces.

Thus far, the film was a fairly Eurocentric, even Anglocentric project, which attempted to combine two strands of critical

Landor Road, from *London* (1994)

thinking. On one hand, there was what one might call the 'urban' literature of Edgar Allan Poe, Charles Baudelaire, Louis Aragon, Walter Benjamin and so on, which had become influential in architectural discourse during the 1970s and '80s, in the context of which London appeared to be a city where certain kinds of urban experience that one might see as characteristic of European cities were difficult, if not impossible, to find. On the other hand were the various 'declinist' scenarios of English capitalism, in particular the idea that England is a backward, failing economy because it has never had a successful bourgeois revolution, and that the City of London's dominance and priorities reinforce this failure. This view was fairly widespread at the time, and was attractive to people in the art and design professions since it offered an explanation (and, in the context of the political 'debate' about the UK's role in Europe, a cure) for the problematic nature of so many aspects of English visual and material culture – the UK's attitude to public space and cities; its apparent inability to produce adequately designed buildings, cars and other consumer goods; its unattractive food and problems with agriculture; the predicament of public services like education and transport; and a whole range of other features of everyday life that might be seen as consequences of laissez-faire.

Alongside these predictable concerns, however, was the awareness that Baudelaire, for instance, was just as fed up with the *quartier latin* as Robinson claimed to be with London. His problem was not really London, but 'The Great Malady, Horror of Home'.[5] Perhaps, one thought, this feeling of *restlessness* that seemed to be so characteristic of life in London was not really such a problem after all. Perhaps it was something to be valued. London might be uncomfortable to live in, but it avoided the more stupefying aspects of *dwelling* that a less spatially impoverished, more 'architectural' city might encourage. Perhaps London was even, despite its obvious anachronisms, rather modern. Even someone as narrow-minded as Robinson could hardly fail to notice the increasingly cosmopolitan make-up of its population.

Without ever really losing sight of its architectural and other preconceptions about London as a physical structure, and with occasional references to the life and work of Baudelaire[6] and Rimbaud, the film explored these ideas in various more or less convincing, sometimes rather touristic, ways, beginning with its narrator's introduction of himself as a returning seaman (albeit only a photographer on a cruise liner). Robinson's first fictional excursion (to Horace Walpole's Strawberry Hill in Twickenham) was provoked by the appearance of a non-fictional Portuguese driving school opposite his flat, one of several new undertakings in the neighbourhood that had accompanied the rapid expansion of the Portuguese community in south Lambeth after Portugal joined the European Union in 1987. By the river in Twickenham, near Alexander Pope's Grotto, the film's protagonists meet two Peruvian musicians, Aquiles and Carlos Justiniani, whose singing accompanied their walk downstream as far as Kew. Aquiles had been actually encountered busking with a colleague in Vauxhall Underground station, and we had arranged to include one of his recordings in the film.

Emerging from the arcades of Brixton market, where he had hoped to confirm a visit by Apollinaire in 1901, Robinson noticed a ship depicted on the sign of The Atlantic, the famous public house opposite, which enabled him to mention the arrival of post-war emigrants from Jamaica on the SS *Empire Windrush*, and the fact that they were initially housed in the deep (air-raid) shelters under Clapham Common. There were similar episodes in cafés and restaurants in the neighbourhoods of Ealing Road, Wembley and Cranford, on the A4 near Heathrow, and a visit to Southall during Diwali. Amid the cultural diversity of Ridley Road market, in Dalston, Robinson 'became much happier and relaxed, and began to talk more positively about London's future', though his companion continued: 'I was not convinced by this: London has always struck me as a city full of interesting people most of whom, like Robinson, would prefer to be elsewhere.' This remark was based on the idea that the actual attainment of a cosmopolitan London was somehow restricted, despite the heterogeneity of its population, either by

Myrtle Avenue, Hatton, from *London* (1994)

spatial characteristics – an emphasis on private, exclusive spaces, perhaps – or by something else. In an interview in Reece Auguiste's film *Twilight City* (Black Audio Film Collective, 1989), Paul Gilroy had spoken of 'an extraordinary change, in which people are able to inhabit the same space, to be physically proximate and yet to live in different worlds'. In the 1980s I had also become used to a characteristically London conversation in which the participants would share their longing to be somewhere else, with each party nostalgic for a different place – the Caribbean, southern Europe, or perhaps a different part of the UK – usually, though not always, somewhere the speaker might regard as *home*.

In the sequence after Ridley Road, Robinson 'discovers' Defoe's house in Stoke Newington, where he wrote most of *Robinson Crusoe*, and London is revealed to him as a place of 'shipwreck, and the vision of Protestant isolation'. Not long after this, during footage of the Notting Hill Carnival and the float of the Colombian Carnival Association, the narrator reads:

He asked me if I found it strange that the largest street festival in Europe should take place in London, the most unsociable and reactionary of cities. I said that I didn't find it strange at all, for only in the most unsociable of cities would there be a space for it, and in any case, for many people London was not at all unsociable.[7]

The suggestion here, and elsewhere in the film, was that there is something about London – some 'absence', perhaps – that makes it easier than it might be elsewhere for incoming cultures to establish themselves, but that perhaps also limits the extent to which London's diverse cultures experience each other.

Towards the end of the film, Robinson makes his way along Fleet Street, where he has to be prevented from attacking the Lord Mayor during a parade, to the portico of the Royal Exchange, outside the Bank of England, where he declares: 'The true identity of London is in its *absence*. As a city, it no longer exists. In this alone it is truly modern: London was the first metropolis to disappear.' I had wondered if the last line of this rhetorical assertion might not exceed the terms of the character's licence, but it did seem to echo something about the state of London as an *idea*. Notions of absence, however, had been implicit in the project from its beginning, whether as 'the absence of Continental diversions', as the idea that London suffered – or benefited – from an absence of a (known) identity, or as an identity that could be characterised as a sense of absence. Apart from these generalisations, there were a number of candidates for specific things that were absent – the memory of the historic centre, for instance, obscured by the increasing blandness of the spaces of the banking and finance industries, which had driven out most other forms of economic activity and were staffed to a great extent by commuters from outside London; the port, and its once-numerous shipping in the river. The absence of metropolitan government, of a credible London newspaper (the *Evening Standard* is read all over the southeast of England), even the lack of topographical logic in London's territorial subdivision into boroughs, all contributed to a sense that Londoners had only a very vague idea of what London was, or

simply did not need to know. Perhaps London's economic dominance makes this unnecessary. In any case, people who have lived
in London all their lives often have only a very limited knowledge
of its topography. A good deal of the above can be dismissed as a
feature of any large capital city, where the national often eclipses
the civic, but anyone who has ever tried to buy a postcard of
London will have noticed that it is a city that lacks a contemporary
self-image.

Such images, in any case, have probably always been mislead-
ing. In the nineteenth century, London's population grew from
about 860,000 in 1801 to 6.5 million in 1901. Although the children of Londoners stood a better chance of surviving than many
elsewhere in the country, most of this increase was the result of
in-migration either from the rest of the UK or abroad. Not only
that, but many migrants did not stay in the city, so the actual
extent of in-migration was even higher than the growth in the
population suggests. A 'typical' Londoner of the nineteenth
century might be imagined, not as a cab-driver or a publican, but
as young, isolated, poor and newly arrived from somewhere else,
probably more so than today. Even now, net migration into
London is principally by people between the ages of fifteen and
twenty-nine.[8]

Similar things can be said of other aspects of English culture.
Leaving aside industrial items such as white bread, gin and sugar
cubes, or niche-market regional revivals, whatever might amount
to an 'English' cuisine, for instance, has been very hard to find
since the decline in the agricultural workforce during the nineteenth and early twentieth centuries, or perhaps for even longer,
since the establishment of national markets centred on London.
Agricultural decline (which was one of the factors that drove
migrants to London) was partly the result of importing cheaper
food, often from Britain's colonies. At the same time, the cuisines
of cultures colonised by the British and others began to find their
way to Britain. The result is that the stereotype of unattractive
'British' food, which is still not difficult to find, contrasts with an
enormous variety of imported and hybrid cuisines that is

probably more extensive than that in places where some kind of indigenous cuisine survives.

It is apparently an assumption of 'classical' economics that a nation, having established some comparative advantage in producing particular goods or services, should strive to import as much of the remainder of its material and other needs as possible. I came across this idea only recently and, to someone who can remember the 1960s, when there seemed to be a near-permanent balance of payments crisis, it came as something of a surprise. I had always thought that an industrial economy's success was more likely to be indicated by the volume and quality of its exports. Culturally, an unwillingness to make things might seem unattractive, but as an indicator of wealth, imports do make sense, given that, in the long run, they confirm the ability of the importing economy to generate the means to pay for them. A high level of imports might therefore be seen to indicate success, rather than failure, and certainly seems to have characterised the UK's economy for long enough for it to be regarded as traditional.

If the everyday experience of London in the early 1990s really was characterised by some more or less definable sense of *absence*, combined with an apparent comparative openness to incoming cultures, perhaps this has something to do with London's or the UK's economy. In a recent essay,[9] the film historian Paul Dave referred to the film *London* in the context of Ellen Meiksins Wood's book *The Pristine Culture of Capitalism* (1991). Having considered the various declinist scenarios of post-war British economic history, Wood asks the question: 'Is Britain, then, a peculiar capitalism or is it peculiarly capitalist?' and argues that it is the latter. She also offers an explanation for what sounds rather like Robinson's 'problem of London':

> What American tourists today think of as the characteristically 'European' charm of the major Continental cities – the cafés, the fountains, the craftsmanship, the particular uses of public space – owes much to the legacy of burgherdom and urban patriciates . . . This kind of urban culture was overtaken very early in England by

the growth of the national market centred in London . . . Today's
urban landscape in Britain – the undistinguished modern architecture, the neglect of public services and amenities from the arts to
transportation, the general seediness – is not an invention of
Thatcherism alone but belongs to a longer pattern of capitalist
development and the commodification of all social goods, just as
the civic pride of Continental capitals owes as much to the tradi-
tions of burgher luxury and absolutist ostentation as to the values
of modern urbanism and advanced welfare capitalism.[10]

This statement locates the origin of London's 'absence of
Continental diversions' in the sixteenth and early seventeenth
centuries, at the time that the English began to colonise other parts
of the world, and it is not difficult to see a propensity for colonisation in 'the commodification of all social goods', as Robinson
Crusoe and his contemporaries in the sugar-growing business
amply demonstrated. The urban landscape that Wood describes,
which is particularly typical of London, can be seen as the current
manifestation of a quality that has endured through pre-colonial,
colonial and post-colonial periods.

What is particularly intriguing about London in 2003, rather
than in 1992, is that the post-colonial, cosmopolitan make-up of
its population is juxtaposed with a physical form that, while it
largely remains in the dilapidated condition to which Wood
alludes, is increasingly the subject of initiatives by people who
might be construed as members of a previously absent 'burgherdom', whose aim is to make urban experience in London more
like that of a certain kind of European city. Examples of this
tendency might include Lord Rogers's Urban Task Force, various
projects of the Architecture Foundation, the RIBA's award of its
Gold Medal to the city of Barcelona in 1999, and the creation of
new and successful public buildings and other spaces, such as
Tate Modern, the London Eye and the central London riverside
generally.

One wonders if the culture that Wood describes, which seems
to be very much a characteristic of the era of colonisation, might

be changing. Latterday burgherdom has emerged in the context of an economy that, while it shows few signs of becoming a European-style social democracy, is now inevitably more closely linked to that of mainland Europe than for several centuries. The call for an urban revival, for example, is underpinned by the idea that, in order to maintain its appeal to the international financial sector, London needs to upgrade its amenities to the level of more civilised European cities. Generally speaking, this project is largely, though not exclusively, the province of a white, well-heeled middle or even ruling (if not exactly *upper*) class; but it does, arguably, represent a commitment to the kind of public and other spaces in which London's potential to become a genuinely cosmopolitan city might be realised.

At the same time, 'regeneration' is both accompanied by and accomplished through the 'discovery' of previously overlooked value in neighbourhoods and property often occupied by the people most characteristic of this cosmopolitan city, who are usually among the first to be pushed out when 'regeneration' occurs and values rise. This point is frequently made, but a more fundamental question might be whether the cultural diversity and richness of old-fashioned, hard-faced London – the London of 'capitalist development and the commodification of all social goods', which is the economic reality from which the present-day post-colonial city has emerged – are actually opposed by the economic and cultural changes that the current attempts at quasi-European make-over arguably exemplify.

If cultural diversity and richness are synonyms for poverty, as to some extent they are, they are almost certainly threatened. In post-regeneration London, for example, the frequently ensuing sterility is perhaps not so much a question of culture as of residential densities. Wealthy, childless couples living in 300-square-metre riverside lofts are unlikely to generate anything like the street life of a community of immigrant families with children, each living in a single room. Diversity and richness, however, will survive in other neighbourhoods. In any case, it is not certain that the make-over, such as it is, is European in character. The pavement cafés of post-1994 London seem to have arrived, not from Europe, but via North America. The evolution of London's population, too, increasingly polarised between extremes of rich and poor, more closely resembles that of North American cities than anything in Europe.

London in 2003 certainly seems to be a more enjoyable place than it was in 1992, in all sorts of ways, but physically it has not changed anything like as much as its stock of recently constructed public buildings might suggest. One of the more striking aspects of the cities of present-day mature economies is how, in the twentieth century, they changed, physically, much less than they might have been expected to at the beginning of the century. Cities now often evolve in ways that involve social change and subjectivity rather more than actual physical alteration. Much of London's physical fabric is older than that of many other cities in Europe, and older than that of much of the rest of the UK. New built environments are usually less socially and economically diverse than older urban fabric, so perhaps the fluidity of London's population is encouraged by this physical stasis – though at a price, since it condemns thousands, if not millions of people to live in unusually impoverished physical surroundings, both public and private. If London really is more open to new possibilities of various kinds than other cities whose urbanism is more conventionally European, its physical shortcomings soon restrict their impact on the general condition of the city. In the long run, London's economy is becoming increasingly specialised (in finance and administration). In this, as so often in the UK and presumably elsewhere, life in London seems to be characterised by predicaments in which a 'yes' is followed by a 'but'.

8

London – Rochester – London

In December 1864, Charles Dickens received a Christmas present from the actor Charles Fechter – a prefabricated two-storey summer house in the form of a Swiss chalet. It was delivered from Switzerland in ninety-four pieces packed in fifty-eight boxes, and was erected in the shrubbery at Gad's Hill Place, Dickens's house near Rochester, in Kent, where he lived from 1856 until his death in 1870. The main coach road from London to Dover ran through Dickens's property and, to reach the shrubbery, he had a tunnel made beneath the road. The upper room in the chalet became Dickens's study, where he wrote parts of the unfinished *Mystery of Edwin Drood*, on which he was working in the chalet the day before he died. On the walls, in the spaces between the windows, Dickens placed five large mirrors, of which he said: 'they reflect and refract, in all kinds of ways, the leaves that are quivering at the windows, and the great fields of waving corn, and the sail-dotted river. My room is up among the branches of the trees.'

Knowing that Cedric Price had appeared in a film that I had made about houses and possessed a video copy of another, the publisher Nick Barley* suggested that we should go on a trip together. He told me that Cedric was keen on Dickens. I suggested

---

* The essay was commissioned for and first published in Hans Ulrich Obrist, ed., *Re:CP* (Basel: Birkhäuser, 2003), a book of projects and texts by Cedric Price, with an interview by Obrist and other texts by Arata Isozaki and Rem Koolhaas.

Dickens's chalet, Rochester, Kent, 2001

the Thames estuary, which I had long associated with various themes – mobility, expendability, non-plan and so on – in the work of Price and some of his contemporaries (and which is featured in both the films already mentioned, partly for this reason). We decided to go to Rochester because of its role in Dickens's first novel *The Pickwick Papers*, and only then discovered that Dickens's chalet is preserved there. It was arranged that Cedric, Nick and I would travel to its present location in the garden of Eastgate House, in Rochester, which is now the Dickens Centre.* Nick was to drive; there was to be no stopping off en route. We would meet at Cedric's office at ten o'clock in the morning, and be back by half-past-four in the afternoon.

Alfred Place

Cedric had been in the office since eight, but had been interrupted by telephone calls. We discussed the pros and cons of various methods of communication. I mentioned that I had recently located a copy of a useful but long out-of-print book in a bookshop only a few minutes' drive from my home with the aid of the Bookfinder website, which led Cedric to suggest *Serious Business*, a book of water-colours by J. H. Dowd, a popular artist of the 1930s, as a test of any such facility.[1] The cover of this cloth-bound book which, he said, contained images of children and sandy beaches, was a particular shade of green favoured by interior decorators of the 1930s, but neither of us could think of the name of the colour.[2] He was about to fetch his watercolours to identify it when Nick arrived, and we set out, in a hired Kia.

---

* The Dickens Centre closed in 2004. In 2010, the Rochester and Chatham branch of the Dickens Fellowship and Medway Council launched a £100,000 appeal to restore the chalet.

Russell Square

I was already suggesting we might manage a detour to Chalk, the village between Gravesend and Rochester where the blacksmith's forge is traditionally the model for that in *Great Expectations*, when Cedric pointed out a truck, which crossed our path as we approached the square, with a single twenty-foot container on the end of its semi-trailer, as a Foden, and we discussed surviving UK and other truck manufacturers.

Guilford Street to Clerkenwell

Back to Chalk, then *hulks* (the prison ships of *Great Expectations*), their location in the river, and the difficulty faced by escaping prisoners in getting off the marshes; Cedric suggested the spatial uses characteristic of the estuary were determined by its potential for *secrecy and security*. We passed the end of Doughty Street, where Dickens lived between 1837 and 1839 at No. 48, now the Dickens House. Seeing a Citroën DS coming the other way, I ventured it was a 'nice car' (Alison Smithson's book *AS in DS* having been republished a few weeks earlier), but this led instead, via the colour of the driver's pullover, which was green, back to *Serious Business*, and whether (or not) it is becoming increasingly difficult to imply nuance in written language in the way this title did in the 1930s (it seems to have become something of a catchphrase).

Old Street roundabout

On the west side of City Road, at its junction with this roundabout (one of the realised fragments of Abercrombie's 1943 plan for London) is a large building with terracotta facing, of mixed, uncertain use, called Imperial Hall, which we all agreed looks as if it might have been misplaced from Manchester, or perhaps Blackpool, or even North America. I suggested that this might be because in these places buildings are allowed to age, whereas in London they are more likely to be subject to continual, often ineffectual refurbishment. In Commercial Street (which fails to confirm this idea), Cedric asked where we were, before recognising the huge redevelopment at Aldgate, circa 1980, as the last built work of the architect Sir Frederick Gibberd.

Commercial Road, East India Dock Road

I had recently looked at a film, *Houses in the Town*, made by the Central Office of Information in 1951, in which Gibberd presents an argument for an urban (as opposed to suburban) quality in new housing development, and which ends with footage of the construction of the Lansbury Estate (the showcase housing project of the Festival of Britain, in Poplar). Gibberd was involved in this, and designed its market square at Chrisp Street, an early example of a pedestrian shopping centre, which we passed a few minutes later. Cedric mentioned Gibberd's book *The Architecture of England from Norman Times to the Present Day*, published by the Architectural Press in 1938. 'I liked him,' he said, adding that Gibberd had been a member of the Communist Party in the 1930s (one might not imagine this from the film, in which he appears the epitome of an affable, pipe-smoking bourgeois) and that his contact with Attlee had helped him get the commission for Heathrow Airport.

Cedric's first visit to London, he said, was to spend a half-day at the Festival of Britain.[3] He had admired Basil Spence's Sea and Ships Pavilion ('the best thing he ever did'), and recalled the Regatta Restaurant's door handles, in the shape of human hands.

The Bridge House, Canning Town

Beside the A13 flyover, on the north side of the road east of the river Lea, this was a music venue of the punk era. Either it's been demolished, or we missed it. I thought, wrongly, that Charlie Kray had once been its landlord. Kray's twin brothers owned Cedric's first office, above corset-makers Sylphide, at 86 George Street, W1. One day they visited, in a big black car with a couple of minders to block the stairs, to suggest he might like to have a look at other premises in Great Portland Street (all this seemingly something to do with Joan Littlewood). Charlie Kray later showed him round this office, which was (much) later occupied by Peter Murray's company Wordsearch, the original publisher of the magazine *Blueprint*.

The Northern Outfall Sewer crosses the A13, overlooked by the ski slope known as the Beckton Alp; East Ham, Barking, Dagenham

More talk of *secrecy and security*: the military, prisons, danger, explosives, criminals; Purfleet – the Admiralty's powder store in the eighteenth century, where Benjamin Franklin's experimental lightning rods were installed during the controversy between Franklin and Benjamin Wilson over the correct design of lightning conductors. Franklin believed that lightning rods should be tall with pointed ends, Wilson (a successful portraitist of the period) that they should be short with ball ends. There was a theatrical demonstration at the Pantheon, then recently built, in Oxford Street (now the site of Marks and Spencer), gutted by a fire in January 1792, the aftermath of which was a watercolour subject for the sixteen-year-old J. M. W. Turner.

There was a very large stack of containers to the north of the road. As a product of the architectural culture of the late 1960s,

I still consider these a photo-opportunity, but Cedric seems to have moved on, or was, perhaps, never that interested in their *appearance.*[4]

Lakeside, Thurrock

In the 1970s, a Mr English, the Essex environmental officer, commissioned Cedric Price Architects to suggest planning proposals for the chalk quarry at Thurrock, later the site of the Lakeside Shopping Centre.

The Queen Elizabeth II Bridge, Dartford; Stone

Joining the M25, we crossed the bridge, remarking how oddly unremarked on it is, for such a large and geographically significant structure. As we approached the centre of the span, a Chinook twin-rotor military helicopter passed above from east to west.

Travellers descending the bridge are faced by a view of a strange, cliff-like brick building suggestive of a nineteenth-century workhouse, or a prison, which turns out to be the Dartford Bridge Hilton (rooms from £99.00 per night, midweek). Wishing to consult the map, we followed a brown sign for a picnic location, took a wrong road, turned in the entrance to the Davanden Boarding Kennels (tel. 01322 222192), and a minute or so later reached a viewpoint looking north across the river, near the village of Stone, Kent (Cedric was born in Stone, Staffordshire). On the top of a wooden pole was a steel basket, which I took to be one of the nationwide chain of beacons erected in 1988 to commemorate the 400th anniversary of the defeat of the Spanish Armada. Both Cedric and Nick seemed incredulous, as it was not even at the highest point of the surrounding landscape, but we were not far from the fort at Tilbury, where Queen Elizabeth I reviewed the army raised to resist the Armada, and where there would probably be another beacon. Cedric, still unconvinced, pointed out that the fleet was then kept at Two Tree Island, between Canvey and Leigh-on-Sea, some distance downriver. Two Tree Island, formerly an Essex County Council landfill site with a large population of Brent Geese, now a nature reserve, had been the site of another Cedric Price Architects project, for a marina in 1972, successfully opposed, at a public enquiry, by the defenders of the geese – hence the nature reserve. I took some photographs, and we left at about 11.30. There was a man in a red Ford Escort van who may have been dead, or merely asleep, and strands of police tape fluttered at the entrance to this touristic location.

Stone, Swanscombe, Northfleet

At the end of the road we had rejoined we found the A226, the old coach road from London to Dover. At the junction is Stone House, a Victorian asylum still in use as a psychiatric hospital, unlike many others visible from the M25 as it circles London. We turned left, and entered the landscape of the former chalk quarries of north Kent, passing a landfill gas burner in a field to the south of the road. At Stone, Cedric pointed out the McDonald's (job vacancies) as a former coaching inn. We continued east, up a hill to the south of which is the huge hole in which is Bluewater, the last out-of-town shopping mall of its era in the UK, built by the Australian developer Lend Lease. We passed flowers placed by the roadside (it is undoubtedly a dangerous road), long walls made of flints, and developers' signs for new housing.[5] At the top of the hill was another coaching inn, a view of a characteristically square-topped north Kent church and, further on, the gigantic cement works at Northfleet, with which Cedric's friend, the late David Allford, who became a partner at the architects Yorke, Rosenberg and Mardall, had been involved.

Gravesend

We pulled off the road into a street called Khartoum Place, and I read out a passage from Conrad's *Heart of Darkness*, including the following:

> We live in the flicker – may it last as long as the old earth keeps rolling! But darkness was here yesterday. Imagine the feelings of a commander of a fine – what d'ye call 'em? – trireme in the Mediterranean, ordered suddenly to the north . . . Imagine him here – the very end of the world, a sea the colour of lead, a sky the colour of smoke, a kind of ship about as rigid as a concertina – and going up this river with stores, or orders, or what you like. Sand-banks, marshes, forests, savages, – precious little to eat fit for a civilised man, nothing but Thames water to drink. No Falernian wine here, no going ashore.[6]

Returning to the road, we passed soldiers in a backstreet, then drove on past Chalk, Dickens's house at Gad's Hill, a bridge over the dual carriageway that leads to the Isle of Grain (the location of, among other things, the fully automated container port Thamesport), and descended to Strood, Rochester Bridge, and the former city. According to Cedric, the appearance of Rochester Castle, which faced us across the river as we came down the hill ('glorious pile – frowning walls – tottering arches – dark nooks – crumbling staircases'[7]) is partly a result of a twelfth-century bishop's melting the lead on the roof, to pour on surrounding attackers.

Before we set out, Cedric had given us photocopied pages (sent by his brother) from J. M. Richards's compression of Nathaniel Lloyd's *History of the English House*, in which is written, beneath a photograph of the keep of Rochester Castle:

> Although the introduction of stone for regular building purposes by the Normans begins the period when examples of domestic

architecture survive, these examples are by no means typical dwellings of the people. Stone was introduced for purposes of fortification. The political organisation of the time demanded a secure nucleus round which each local feudal unit could gather itself; and the typical surviving Norman building, excluding ecclesiastical buildings, is therefore the castle, which combined the functions of a dwelling-place for a lord and his retainers with that of a fortress. For many years following the Conquest it had to be strong enough to resist attacks by any rebellion of the Saxons. The peasant's dwelling meanwhile remained the primitive hut of wattle and daub or rough timber with thatched roof.

This traditional English scenario contrasts with that of the surprisingly unfortified Roman villa, suggesting that, despite Conrad's worries, the class relations of the Roman occupation were, in the end, more peaceable than those of later periods.

Rochester

From the car park we had thought nearest, we walked along the High Street in the direction of Eastgate House, the route of Chaucer's pilgrims, passing an unrivalled succession of historic buildings, not much altered since the eighteenth century. The Watts Charity Hospital dates from 1579, but is re-fronted. There is a plaque, which we read, which states that the house is the foundation of Richard Watts (d.1599), and that he left funds for the relief of 'six poor travellers, not being rogues or proctors' (proctor: 'person managing causes in court that administers civil or canon law').

Further along, there is a shop that sells souvenir and otherwise collectable china, in the window of which were displayed (as there were when I had last stood there in 1990, and probably will be for many years to come) a selection of plates bearing images of historic military aircraft, and four which together made up a seascape depicting a flotilla of small boats leaving Dover for

Dunkirk in 1940, in which Cedric immediately recognised a Vosper-Thorneycroft air-sea rescue launch. Also in this window were various items of crockery of the green colour that we had been unable to name. I said that I once owned a teapot of this colour, one of the Woods Ware range 'Beryl' – at which Cedric revealed that his mother's maiden name was Woods, of this pottery manufacturing family. He recalled the Crown Hotel, in Stone, where Stalin's successor Malenkov spent his first night outside the Soviet Union. The hotel is in the High Street, where the painter Peter de Wint was born above the butcher's. Cedric's father, an architect, designed the Blackpool Odeon, and another in Hanley, when working for the practice of Harry Weedon. His brother David Price, who had supplied us with a quantity of information about Rochester, is also an architect. Like Sherlock Holmes, Cedric has a *brother*.

The Swiss Chalet

Vivienne Lower, senior custodian of the Dickens Centre, showed us the Chalet. She ascended the external stair, followed by Cedric, and unlocked the door to the upper room, which was a little difficult to open, the weather having been very wet. The building's exterior is, or at least appears, very recently painted, practically as new, but the interior is beautifully aged in surface and odour, and surprisingly dry. The smell was that of sun-warmed, tongue-and-groove pine interiors not often opened to the outside air – summer houses, boat sheds and so on. The furniture more or less matches, but is not original. I photographed the stand-in for Dickens's waste-paper basket, and made some attempts at portraiture.

The room is about four metres square and, I guessed, perhaps three high. We discussed the mirrors. Cedric asserted the superiority, at least in this context, of virtual space over actual space, but I was trying to frame a picture without appearing in it in a mirror, and missed the rest of this. He had recently addressed a conference on virtual reality, in Berlin. We agreed that Dickens would have enjoyed the juxtaposition of actual views through the windows and virtual views in the mirrors, perhaps more than being merely surrounded by windows.

There is an essay by Eisenstein setting out the similarities between Dickens's narratives and the forms of early Soviet cinema. Eisenstein, it seems, regarded Dickens as the pioneer of montage.[8] I had never followed up this aspect of Dickens, who was, with a number of other English-language writers (such as Oscar Wilde and Laurence Sterne) sometimes misunderstood in England, *big in* (revolutionary) *Russia*. While I knew of Sterne's influence on the Russian Formalists, I had never previously read *The Pickwick Papers* but, having discovered Cedric's enthusiasm for it, by the day of our journey had reached Chapter 8. Like Sterne's *Tristram Shandy*, it is much influenced by Cervantes's *Don Quixote*, and in Chapter 50 of *Pickwick*, Dickens has Sam Weller allude to Sterne's *Sentimental Journey*.

I had not realised how close *Pickwick* is to the eighteenth century, both in its date and in the innovative structures of its narrative. It was Dickens's first novel, set in 1827 and written and published, as a commissioned serial, in 1836–37, when he was only twenty-four. It was, on the other hand, the product of a nineteenth-century technological revolution, that of mass-produced, cheap paper, and was a runaway commercial success – so much so that, within the period of its serialisation, Pickwick soaps and Weller corduroys were on sale, and portraits of 'Boz' appeared on London omnibuses.

Cedric, on the other hand, had not read much Sterne, and we were retracing *Pickwick*'s exploration of a period which, while pre-Victorian, is long past the beginning of the nineteenth century. The slightly later period, when Dickens was writing, is that of Marc Brunel's Thames Tunnel (his son Isambard narrowly survived an accident working on this in 1827); the first railways (Euston Station opened in 1836); mains gas for cooking and lighting (the Bankside Gas Works was built in 1815); the first suburban cemeteries (Kensal Green opened in 1833); and the first mass-media. Amid this modernity, London's population, just under a million in 1800, had reached 1.8 million in 1840, and the city was still much smaller than what might be conventionally termed 'Victorian' London.

Nick compared the chalet's lightness to the traditional gloom of the Victorian domestic interior. Cedric pointed out that sunlight was, at the time, a recognised cure for killer illnesses (Dickens was already in poor health when he received the chalet); the Victorians' love of views, and the romance of strange sights and strange places. Dickens visited Switzerland in 1844 and 1846, and by 1865, Davos, with its landscape of chalets, was established as a cure for tuberculosis and other respiratory diseases (in 1881 Robert Louis Stevenson would visit, and in 1893 Louisa Conan Doyle). Cedric compared the chalet with Queen Victoria's summer house at Frogmore. Even in the twentieth century, he added, TB was still a killer in Britain: two of his uncles died of the disease. (His Uncle Charles, who designed furniture for Heal's, sending money home to his family, died in the YMCA, in Great Russell Street.)

After Dickens's death, the chalet was dismantled by Mr J. Couchman, a Strood master builder, who had originally erected it, and re-erected at the Crystal Palace, Sydenham, before being moved, again by Mr Couchman, to the grounds of Cobham Hall, as a gift to Lord Darnley from the Dickens family. By 1961 it was deteriorating, and was rescued by the Dickens Fellowship, who presented it to the (Rochester) City Council.

We left Eastgate House and walked back along the High Street towards the bridge, which replaces that on which Mr Pickwick stood looking at the view when invited to consider whether 'drowning would be happiness and peace'. I asked Cedric how the virtual reality conference in Berlin had gone (it had gone very well). We passed the Corn Exchange, where the clock was donated, in 1706, by Sir Cloudesley Shovel, who I knew only from the sign of a public house in Liverpool Road, Islington, near Cloudesley Square, but who was, it states beneath the clock, MP for Rochester in three parliaments in the reign of William III, and in another in that of

Queen Anne. Nick suggested, rather suddenly, that the clock was a phallic symbol. Cedric recalled an account of Shovel's death at the hands of a woman who murdered him for his ring, but said he didn't know Liverpool Road, and that there were many parts of London which he had never been to. We approached the Royal Victoria and Bull Hotel, which is the original of the Bull Inn in *The Pickwick Papers*.

The Bull Inn

Beneath the archway, to the right, there was an Italian restaurant, which we passed up. We tried the hotel entrance to the left and, finding it unattended, continued to the bar, which was empty of customers but staffed by two sympathetic young women. A bottle of wine not being available, we bought, in unconscious homage to *Pickwick*, one hot brandy-and-water and two half-pints of Guinness (porter), sat down at a table by the window, and ordered what were arguably *sandwiches*.[9] While the others were looking at the menu, I read the notices displayed in the street door lobby:

Rochester Pub Watch
WARNING
If you commit any offence you will be immediately
barred from all licenced premises in the area.
Proof of age may be required.

Pickwick notes, of Rochester:

> The streets present a lively and animated appearance, occasioned chiefly by the conviviality of the military . . . It was but the day before my arrival, that one of them had been most grossly insulted in the house of a publican. The bar-maid had positively refused to draw him any more liquor; in return for which, he had (merely in playfulness) drawn his bayonet, and wounded the girl in the

shoulder. And yet this fine fellow was the very first to go down to the house next morning, and express his readiness to overlook the matter, and forget what had occurred![10]

Cedric was trying to remember the name of a coaching inn in London, which he thought appeared in *Pickwick*, in which the cellars, later in the nineteenth century, could accommodate 2,000 horses. I had recently learnt (from a radio discussion about biodiesel) that before the petrol engine, about 26 per cent of agricultural land was devoted to growing food for horses. Was the inn called the Star? It was destroyed early on in the Blitz. His mother had owned a car called a Star before the war, built in Solihull. They lived at Studland, in Dorset, in Agglestone Road. His father was in the marines, having been in the Navy in the First World War, and was at Scapa Flow.

We talked about Shovel, about Rochester's wealth (in Dickens, it is still a bit brash) and about the Georgian Navy, 'the largest industrial unit of its day in the western world'; of the decline of timber building in Britain, and the shortage of timber caused by the growth in iron-making. The *Agamemnon*, Nelson's flagship at the Battle of the Nile, had been the last warship built in the New Forest shipyard at Buckler's Hard. Cedric referred to a (technological) time lag that sometimes exists between England and mainland Europe, as with, for example, the import of bricks and tiles from Holland. He recalled the Soupçon restaurant in Hastings, built with ship's timbers recovered, he conjectured, from a ship wrecked on the nearby Goodwin Sands.

West Green

Still in Dorset, I mentioned Patrick Wright's books on Tyneham and the tank, which I had recently read, and that J. F. C. Fuller, the evangelist of tank warfare, had previously been involved with Aleister Crowley. When at Cambridge, Cedric had borrowed a couple of pages of Crowley's diary from Tom Driberg, and published it in an article by Nicholas Tomalin in *Granta*, under the title 'Favourite Eccentrics', which led us, via Rabelais's 'Do what you will', to West Green House – built by Henry 'Hangman' Hawley (who commanded the cavalry at Culloden) – the former home of Cedric's friend Alistair, Lord McAlpine.

An article in the *Sunday Times*, not long before the 1997 election, described parties at West Green:

> The guests were not just prominent Tories but also artists, dealers, writers and stalwart socialists. One of McAlpine's closest friends, the architect Cedric Price, has been on the left of the Labour Party since he was 16. He says: 'I feel I've been in an occupied country under the Tories in the last 18 years. But I don't care about Alistair's politics – I think he's a great man.'

Cedric recalled a Christmas at the house; McAlpine was in Venice, and had lent him the keys. His (Cedric's) sister came from Shetland dressed as a witch, his brother David as Long John Silver, and David's wife as a penguin. The witch was later seen begging in the woods. He recalled their childhood home in Staffordshire. Staffordshire, he said, does everything by halves,[11] adding, in the context of country houses, via Shugborough and Ingestre Hall in Staffordshire, that Wren built only one country house, Winslow Hall, in Buckinghamshire, not far from Stowe. Wren, he argued, as a scientist, was a more significant figure than Hawksmoor, who was the better architect.

Bath chaps

On a visit to Sheffield, Jeremy Till, the head of Sheffield University's school of architecture, had recommended a visit to Castle Market, a building admired by Cedric who, he said, had gone there to buy Bath chaps, but neither Jeremy nor I knew what a Bath chap was. Castle Market was completed in the early 1960s, designed by the City Architect's department under Lewis Womersley. It is a unique, multi-levelled interior, its viability now threatened by the mall at Meadowhall. A Bath chap is a kind of fast food: a pig's cheek, cooked. They can be bought in Bath, and in Castle Market, Sheffield (and perhaps elsewhere), but in Sheffield, they come with the jawbone, including the teeth.

Cedric once hosted breakfast, at his office, for David Allford, Bryan Henderson (also of YRM) and Alistair McAlpine. McAlpine was to bring Bath chaps, but arrived with grouse, 'looking like the president of the Maidenhead yacht club' in someone else's clothes. He had set fire to West Green cooking the Bath chaps, as is traditional, over candles. The house was gutted.

The nineteenth century

I asked Cedric whether, given the choice, he would have preferred to live in the eighteenth century or the nineteenth. In the nineteenth century, he said, everything was up for grabs, for invention: custard powder, Carter's Liver Pills, Beecham's Powders. The eighteenth century, on the other hand, was the century of slavery, of an old, Classical idea of knowledge, and established reason. He cited Dickens's admiration for America.

London

One of the factors in our choice of destination had been the predicament of the Thames estuary, and of north Kent in particular, as one of the few places (perhaps the only place) in the UK where a new landscape is being created. This involves both the construction of the Channel Tunnel and its rail link, and the related project for the regeneration of the estuary – the *Thames Gateway* ('Heseltine's Valhalla in the east', Cedric called it, later) – an attempt to balance, or even reverse, the westward drift of London's prosperity and the pull of Heathrow Airport.[12] In the last few decades, however, the UK's east coast ports have grown much more than

those on the west coast, partly as a result of increased trade with
Europe, but perhaps more because of their proximity to the world's
largest port, Rotterdam. I asked Cedric if he thought it was possible to reverse centuries of westward drift in London. Without
rejecting it, he didn't seem to accept the generality of westward
drift, and suggested instead that the future of London was more
likely to be determined by its position on the map of interconti-
nental air travel. Once again, Cedric referred to the English Channel
as a time warp, and to Dutch faience. It was never quite clear, he
said, whether the Channel was a thoroughfare, or something to be
crossed. On the map of air routes, London was out on a limb. In
the long run, Paris might overtake Heathrow, and London face the
prospect of decline, just as Liverpool, once the major European
north Atlantic port, and a world city, had done before it.

Blue Bell Hill

We drove to the M2 junction at Blue Bell Hill, south-east of the town,
to see the Channel Tunnel Rail Link under construction. Cedric
recalled the project for the Solway Barrage, whose protagonist, Dr
Robert Drew, had commissioned his computer centre for the British
Transport Docks Board, near Heathrow, in 1967. Cedric had had
some involvement with London and Continental Railways, who are
responsible for building the link between the tunnel and Ebbsfleet.

Cross-channel rail traffic is not new. Until quite recently, train
ferries still ran between Dover and Dunkirk – 29,000 rail wagons in
1994. In Dover's Western Docks, where the Dunkirk ferry berthed,
there was formerly a bar, The Golden Arrow, named after the
passenger service which ran between London and Paris. I asked
Cedric if he had ever travelled on the *Golden Arrow*. In 1953, he
said, on his way to Venice: 'I liked Venice, when I went, but it was
very smelly.' He sold a lot of drawings. 'My dad had just died, so it
was quite a rough time.'

As we drove back to London, he remarked on the extent of
countryside he doesn't know, because he doesn't drive. When we

reached Blackheath, where his brother lives, and where Tom Driberg lived at the Paragon, there was a Chinook, perhaps the same
one we'd seen earlier, following the river.

In Rotherhithe, I said I'd only recently learnt that Marc Brunel
was French, and that, in Plymouth for the car ferry, I had seen the
Saltash railway bridge, for the first time. We all admired this bridge,
completed in 1859. Cedric asked what sort of car ferry leaves from
Plymouth. He doesn't spend much time in France, he said, but was
interested in Portugal.

Crossing Tower Bridge, we saw Norman Foster's Greater
London Assembly building, under construction, overlooking the
river. 'It's not very big, is it?' I said. Cedric had recently been having
a look round 'with Paul Finch, and his instant camera', when Max
Neal, Foster's project architect, who used to work in Cedric's office,
had spotted them. He would have laid something on, he said, if
he'd known they were coming. Cedric thought it was good to have
a small building for the GLA. 'Keep it small, like a cartoon.' (A
small city, he said, not like 'Heseltine's Valhalla in the east'.)

A few minutes later, we passed the Richard Cloudesley School
(in Golden Lane), then Ron Herron's GLC school (at the corner of
Gray's Inn Road and Sidmouth Street, now part of Westminster
Kingsway College).* On the opposite side of Sidmouth Street
there is, I learnt, an experiment in brick and concrete panel prefab-
rication, an estate of flats built in the early 1950s. At about five
o'clock, the car pulled up near Cedric's office, and we went our
separate ways.

---

* Since demolished.

9

The Robinson Institute

Most of us spend much of our time in spaces made and previously occupied by other people, usually people of the more or less distant past. We might reasonably expect our everyday surroundings to feel haunted but, by and large, they don't. Haunting is still relatively unusual. We all live, as far as we know, in the present, and the present in Nepal, in Tokyo, or on Mars, can sometimes seem nearer than yesterday morning in one's own kitchen. As it has become easier to move around in and communicate across space, have we, perhaps, become more sensitive to the fact that we are inescapably stranded, shipwrecked almost, in our own present, and are we therefore increasingly attracted to the idea of time travel?

I can remember, a few years ago, trying to imagine how subjective experience of space might change as a result of one's connection to the internet. For a long time, it had seemed that the spaces of everyday surroundings – the home, the high street and so on – were becoming more marginal in character, compared with other spaces that might be thought typically modern, or postmodern – the airport, the office tower, the big museum and so on. Local spaces, at least in the UK, then appeared, as they still appear, to be suffering a general decline: in the disempowerment of local government, for example; from physical dilapidation and decay, as trends in the wider economy make small-scale maintenance and repair of ordinary buildings increasingly problematic; and in a variety of other ways. A large proportion of housing, in particular

– especially private-sector rented housing – appeared, and still appears, to be in very poor condition.

I had wondered whether the increasing scope and availability of new technology, especially mobile communications technology, would make any difference to the apparently marginal character of much everyday experience, especially urban experience. For much of the twentieth century, artists, writers and revolutionaries had attempted to deal with this and similar predicaments by employing more or less explicit strategies to poeticise or otherwise transform experience of everyday surroundings. The Surrealists and their followers were probably the leading exponents of this, and the Surrealist encounter with everyday experience generally involved the cultivation of subjectivities that revealed previously unappreciated value and meanings in ordinary things. The found object, being portable, is the most familiar result of this revelatory process, but the Surrealists also discovered examples of found architecture and found space. Photography, in the most general way, has also offered similar transformations since its invention. In life, this kind of experiential change, which sometimes involves a heightened awareness of events and appearances not unlike that produced by certain drugs, is (in the absence of continuous revolution) generally ephemeral; but in art, literature, cinema and so on, such glimpses, conventionally experienced in isolation, or perhaps with another or others to whom one is very close, can be reconstituted and shared with a suitably receptive viewer, reader or audience. Edgar Allan Poe's story 'The Man of the Crowd' offers an early prototype for this kind of modernist *flâneur* text, and was written at about the time when the modern paradox of visibility and isolation – the convention of silence in public between strangers – was beginning to dominate in cities such as Paris and London.

In the early 1990s, it had seemed to me that the growth of virtual space, and the migration into it of all kinds of economic activity, would speed the decline of some kinds of actual, public space. The closing of bank premises was sometimes referred to as an example of this trend, banking activities being increasingly conducted via cash machines, and by post or telephone. With only slight exaggeration, one could imagine that in some kinds of public space – the less frequented streets of the City of London, say – the sense of their being conventionally public places had all but disappeared, there being so few people about outdoors; while indoors, people were more likely to be peering into the virtual space of their computer screens than looking out of the window. These exterior spaces seemed to be developing something of the feel of other kinds of space that, while not inaccessible, are largely hidden from view – the space behind a television, perhaps, or on top of a wardrobe. In the rural landscape, too, there was a similar quality. With a bit of effort, one could imagine that parts of it were as unexperienced as if they were merely access space for the maintenance engineers of mobile telephone networks.

By the mid 1990s however, it appeared that this new aridity, while it undoubtedly existed, was not all that widespread. I had noticed that our local high street, for example, despite its increasing dilapidation, was a site of still-flourishing economic activity and increasingly visible global connectedness. The newsagent's window displayed cards offering cut-price telephone deals to many distant territories. Other shops offered cheap flights, both to emigrant and tourist destinations. New 'ethnic' restaurants and shops were opening all the time, most recently (then) a Russian delicatessen. It also turned out to be the locale of an internationally successful pop group. In many ways, this local, physically decaying space was more pervasively and successfully *global* than the average airport, and certainly much more so than the nearby business park, built on what was previously the site of a car factory, and owned by the property development subsidiary of British Aerospace, which I had been previously inclined to read as a typical spatial outcome of the contemporary economy, and was certainly characterised by the aridity previously identified, despite its electric fountains.

Perhaps the condition of the *local* was beginning to evolve in a different, more positive way. Perhaps we were on the verge of a new, electronic *flânerie*, in which experience of place was enhanced by the possibility of immediate connection, via the virtual realm, to people, both friends and strangers, in other places. Perhaps the era of visibility and isolation, of silence between strangers in public, was coming to an end. Perhaps these new predicaments would give rise to a kind of radical subjectivity, which might even be less ephemeral than those of the Surrealists, the Situationists or their latterday adherents, and would somehow install itself in the street, transcending its marginality and dilapidation. For some reason, I first encountered these thoughts while riding a bicycle. For a week or so afterwards, I experienced a mild e-euphoria, a quasi-surrealist frisson, though when I finally got round to signing up with Demon (then a leading provider), this soon disappeared. A few years later, however, many of the former banks that briefly exemplified the evacuation of economic activity from the high street have reopened as bars,[1] and in most of them there are people talking on mobile phones. A kind of electronic *flânerie* has arrived, though, as with so many predicted phenomena, not in quite the way it was anticipated.

One of the internet's most intriguing capabilities, for a topographical film-maker, was that it offered contemporaneous views of distant landscapes. During 1996, I had heard that there were websites where one could access the cameras that observe traffic on UK motorways, and immediately conceived a strong desire to explore, and perhaps to sample, what I imagined would be a large and increasing number of real-time moving images of landscapes throughout the world. I wondered if perhaps, one day, I might be able to make a film without having to leave the house. In fact, at the time, there seemed to be hardly any real-time outdoor web cameras operating anywhere in the world – most of the topographical camera sites only offered a still, updated daily or perhaps hourly, or not at all – but somehow the scarcity of this imagery, its poor resolution, and the way that the images trickled, very slowly, into the monochrome screen of my already obsolete PowerBook made it all the more attractive. In the house in which we then lived, the telephone socket was in the kitchen, and I used to let the pictures load while I was doing the washing up. I never found any views of UK motorways.

The first site I came across that offered anything approaching real-time moving pictures was that of a company called Actual Size

Internet Solutions, who had a camera in a first-floor office over-looking Trinity Square, Colchester, in Essex. This showed a fresh still every two or three seconds, and was particularly impressive at night, when occasional figures passing along the pavement suggested an Essex *noir*. The site became briefly newsworthy when it was revealed that the Neuhoff family, formerly of New Mexico, had moved to Colchester as a result of having seen it, attracted by the apparent absence of crime. They were not, they said, disappointed by the reality of the town, despite its garrison of 4,000 soldiers, and streets patrolled by military police.

Another early favourite was a camera at Mawson Station, an Australian research base in Antarctica. To begin with, this was a single image of the station, updated every hour. If it was dark, as it often was, the screen was black. If it was daylight, with a blizzard, it was white or grey. At other times, there was a view of huts, sometimes illuminated. It didn't occur to me at the time, but I suspect that part of the attraction of this view was the ease with which one could misconstrue it as a window looking into another time. Mawson Station is named after Sir Douglas Mawson, whose Australasian Antarctic Expedition was undertaken in the years 1911–14, and the rudimentary monochrome images were not unlike those of polar explorations of the period. They also evoked the *décor* of the Howard Hawks-produced film *The Thing from Another World* (1951).

The name of Mawson was familiar as that of the designer of Stanley Park, in Blackpool, who quoted the remark of an unidentified Lancashire businessman: 'Blackpool stands between us and revolution'.[2] Stanley Park in Blackpool is named after a member of the family of the Earls of Derby, other members of which have given their name to Stanley Park in Liverpool and Stanley Park in Vancouver (and Port Stanley in the Falkland Islands, which is not so far from Antarctica). I had visited the latter Stanley Park in 1994, in Vancouver for the film festival, and been fascinated by the view from its beach of English Bay, where there are nearly always twelve ships lying at anchor, waiting to enter the port. It is said that if there are fewer than twelve ships in English Bay, people in

Vancouver worry. Searching for an image of the bay and its ships I encountered, instead, recorded sounds: one of the park's Nine O'Clock Gun, another of a floatplane taking off from the harbour, like one I had photographed when I was there. There were a number of other sites on the Pacific coast – a view, from a first-floor window, of the car park of a scientific institution in Alaska; a view of the sea transmitted by a Santa Cruz *fogcam*, and a *baycam* in San Diego, which first offered an image of the bay, then another of the airport – all of which recalled the eeriness of a few jet-lagged days in autumn three years earlier. Once again, more or less contemporaneous views of distant places seemed to bring with them the suggestion that it was possible to see across time. One night, just after midnight, I came across Camera 58 of the Freeway Management System of the Arizona Department of Transportation, with an image of Phoenix that was presumably the most Hitchcockian of these metaphysical spaces, but when I tried to revisit the site a few days later, I couldn't find it.

As the months passed, websites generally grew bigger and more cumbersome, the PowerBook became more and more ill suited to these *plongeur* excursions, and I abandoned the habit. A few months later we moved house, and shortly afterwards bought an iMac. The telephone point was no longer in the kitchen, the images were colour and much faster-loading, and the dish-watery, time-suspended ambience of the previous situation was lost. In any case, when I attempted to revisit them, some of the sites had gone, while others had become more extensive and hence, often, less mysterious.

By this time, I had begun work on a film about the present-day predicament of the *house*. This had been under development for some time, and had arisen as a kind of pendant to its predecessor,[3] which had, for reasons I could never quite fathom, largely avoided domestic space. While photographing it, however, my colleague and I had been faced, nearly every night, with the vexed question of where to stay. One night, after a particularly bad experience, we found ourselves in one of a rapidly growing chain of what were, in effect, motels, which had opened during the previous week.[4] We were, the receptionist told us, the first people ever to occupy our rooms. These were large, well furnished and equipped, warm and comfortable, with a decor which, while not entirely sympathetic, was a great deal less disconcerting than that of most of the other places we had stayed in. Before going to sleep, I turned on the television, on which there appeared an image of some young people playing music, one of them, seen in close-up, on a Fender Stratocaster. Musing on the beauty of this instrument, which I had long considered a key twentieth-century artefact, I came to the conclusion that an economy that offers an adolescent the opportunity to own such a guitar, and hence the life-changing possibility of becoming a half-decent imitator of Jimi Hendrix, for less than a couple of hundred pounds (my possibly low estimate of the then-current price of a mass-produced Stratocaster), and that could produce, in the UK, a brand new hotel bedroom of the quality of the one I was then occupying, capable of accommodating a family of five (as we later proved, returning from a day trip to Blackpool) for only £34.50 per night, could not be entirely bad. With this epiphany began a flirtation with consumerism which lasted for a couple of years. What would happen, I thought, if the capabilities of globalised, automated production and distribution, which were held to have made possible what people then sometimes referred to as *the consumer revolution*, could be applied to the production of domestic space, to *housing*?

A couple of years later, the Tories had been swept from office, and the nation was led by a man who not only owns, but apparently plays, a Fender Stratocaster. A few weeks after our night in Wigan, we had stayed in a Forte Travelodge – the rival brand – in the future prime minister's Sedgefield constituency, and discovered a metal plaque which recorded that, earlier in the year, he had officiated at its opening. In the following year, Forte were taken over by Granada, whose chief executive, Gerry Robinson, subsequently appointed by the incoming government as chairman of the Arts Council of England, had stated that Forte's brands were 'under-priced'. As a result, perhaps, of Robinson's intervention, the UK's two rival motel chains no longer offer the emancipatory, bargain-price mobility they did in 1995, and can now be perceived as, sadly, just another aspect of *rip-off Britain*.

The idea that new technology might be about to have some impact on housing, which had occurred to me, had also occurred to others. In the spring of 1996, the architectural press reported a number of initiatives by architects and others which set out to encourage reform of the UK's unloved house-building industry, with references to post-war prefabs, Japanese factory-built houses, car production, and other industrial technologies. It was not difficult to detect the expectation that such projects might flourish under an incoming Labour government. In other parts of the world, notably Japan and North America, computer-aided manufacturing techniques had already been employed, in a variety of ways, in the production of housing. It seemed merely a matter of time before some global corporate initiative began to shake up, buy up or eliminate the UK's house-building industry, either with or without such new technology, in an echo of what had happened to the UK-owned car industry in the early 1970s. There were a number of more or less likely suspects. These included Toyota, by no means the biggest producer of factory-built houses in Japan, but a familiar name; Hutchison Whampoa, who own the port of Felixstowe and had co-founded the Orange mobile phone network, and were already involved with various developments of luxury apartments in central London; Lend Lease, the Australian developer who subsequently realised Bluewater, the last UK shopping mall of its era in the UK, and were planning large new housing developments in its vicinity; and IKEA, who were reported, wrongly, to be developing 'flat-pack' houses to sell for £7,500.

At the same time, travelling up and down the A40, Western Avenue, in London, I had been struck by the dilapidation of many of its 1930s houses. I read a study, funded by the Joseph Rowntree Foundation, which had drawn attention to the very low rate at which dwellings were being replaced in the UK (implying a future lifespan for the average house of several thousand years) and had detailed the extraordinary inadequacies of the industries that maintain, repair and 'improve' existing owner-occupied dwellings. What,

I began to wonder, will become of the millions of ageing dwellings in the UK, if they can be neither replaced nor adequately maintained? I finished the *Robinson* film, and returned to a house full of half-unpacked cardboard boxes and piles of film cans, overcrowded, poorly decorated and furnished, my lover and our children the victims of a neglect of actual space that frequently afflicts people who give too much of their attention to a quality of space found only in films.

Having briefly reconsidered it, as at similar moments during the preceding decades, we set aside the idea of building a *house of the future* to live in (too slow, too psychologically risky: as Nietzsche remarks, 'a truly modern person who wants to build a house has the feeling that he is entombing himself in a mausoleum'). Instead, I imagined a project in which the production of a film might include the realisation of a 'concept' house, designed (as a film set, avoiding the need to secure planning permission and the various other traumas that accompany house-building in real life) either by me or, more likely, an established avant-garde architect. If we could find somewhere to put this, which seemed extremely unlikely, we might subsequently acquire it as a by-product of the production, but would move, in the meantime, to a more generous ready-to-wear dwelling, new or second-hand.

Several years later, we live in a more spacious house, built in 1902, in which I spend most of my waking life working in a room on the first floor overlooking the back garden. This backs on to the gardens of some houses in a neighbouring street, a few doors along from which live a couple who came round once to ask if we knew who owns the overgrown wilderness which backs onto their garden, which is the fenced-off gardens of a pair of large dilapidated houses, formerly a 'hotel', owned by one of the neighbourhood's more notorious and insolent slum landlords – one of several who have, in recent years, rapidly expanded their unrestrained, super-profitable exploitation of the public sector's inability to cope with its responsibilities towards the increasing number of people in the city who find themselves in desperate housing circumstances. Before explaining this, I felt it necessary to say that, if they had seen me looking out of the window through binoculars in the direction of their house, I had been looking, not at them, but at the birds in our garden, in which we are extremely interested, and which have from time to time included goldcrests, blackcaps, goldfinches, long-tailed tits and, unhappily, a sparrow-hawk. They said that they too sometimes watched the birds through binoculars, and he left his card, illustrated with an image of a pen and a bottle of ink, from which I inferred he was a writer. About eighteen months later, I came across a large pile of books in Tesco, in the high street, in which were several copies of his latest 601-page novel, published by Hodder, two for £5.99. Opposite Tesco are the corner-shop premises of an even more aggressive private landlord. The floor level behind the counter is raised, and cars are parked in the narrow space between the pavement and the shop windows, as if those inside were expecting ram-raiders.

All I have to show for the last couple of years are a collection of essays like this one, and a television documentary[5] which is, so far, the only realised fragment of the previously imagined project. Five years after embarking on this, after a second UK election during which housing was scarcely mentioned, there are few signs that any combination of computers, globalised production and consumer pressure is likely to lead to better, cheaper housing. New technology appears to stimulate demand, but does very little to improve supply – as in San Francisco, for example, where the rapid growth of the e-economy was accompanied by a house-price boom. The subsequent bursting of this bubble presumably had the opposite result, so that the overall effect may not only be to inflate prices, but also to increase market turbulence. Meanwhile, the *moment* of consumerism that inspired my project and its contemporaries seems to have passed. Instead of the housing market becoming more like a consumer market, some consumer markets have become more like the housing market, as manufacturers (of toys, for instance, or computer games) and others have remembered how to manipulate scarcity.

There are ten interviews in the film, with academics, architects, a manufacturer (the design engineer James Dyson), and the head of research at FPD Savills, the international property consultants. Setting these up involved a certain amount of e-mail, in which I explained what the film was supposed to be about, asked preliminary questions, and reconsidered the project in the light of the answers. This was the beginning of life as a *tele-cottager*.

The narrative was only partly autobiographical. It was conceived as the document of a fictional researcher, with the voice of Tilda Swinton, who returns to the UK after twenty years 'among a little-known nomadic people of the Arctic, who devote much of their time to the construction of enormous houses made of snow that cost nothing and are frequently rebuilt' to investigate 'the predicament of the house in the United Kingdom' for her employer, an unnamed research organisation. Setting up 'a small research establishment' in 'a large Edwardian house on the outskirts of a provincial university city', she works in an office overlooking the back garden. At a particularly difficult moment towards the end of editing the film, I decided it was no longer a good idea to expect the production of a television programme to be the sole means of realising a quasi-academic project, and have since become an outstation of an academic institution, with a brief to research 'representational space, and the future of the built environment'.

This semi-fictional reconfiguration of one's dwelling as a *think-tank* might seem an extreme reaction to the marginal predicament of domesticity, but it is not so different to the position of many households for whom the telephone, the computer and so on offer unprecedented levels of connectedness to life outside the house. While portable communication has permitted a kind of *flânerie* outdoors, the effects of electronic virtuality on domestic space seem to be more subtle. If my experience is anything to go by (which it may not be, as there are several alternative explanations), these include a renewed appreciation of ordinary, everyday phenomena. Photography, or the Surrealists' frisson, or some drugs, revealed things *as they could be*, but two-way electronic connectedness seems to enrich experience of things *as they are*. This is perhaps partly because, as an individual, one feels less isolated at home, but is also because the virtual spaces of digital communications, unlike those of photography, are not particularly attractive, so that in contrast even the most untidy and unromantically dilapidated interior can sometimes appear to have a lucidity approaching that of a Vermeer. Being, in this way, happier at home, I have noticed that in recent years I have become less keen to travel. There are several other possible explanations for this – the difficulty of getting about as a family of five; meanness, following travel paid for by employers, etc.; a concern not to accumulate images for which I have no immediate use, and so on. In the end, however, I think it is the symptom of a more serious discontent, which is the feeling that, wherever you go, it's always *now*.

The idea that it might be possible to visit other times, rather than merely other places, first arose during the previously mentioned visits to virtual Antarctica, and was revived during the later lengthy preoccupation with the age and likely future of the built environment. While rewriting the *house* film's narration, in the light of perplexing comment from the client, I sometimes entertained *bad thoughts* towards my producers (there were two, which I imagine is never a good idea). I would wake early, often in the middle of the night, and got into the habit of reading Dickens's *Bleak House* to pass the hours until morning. I had not read the book before, but had owned an audiobook version, read by Paul Scofield, for several years. I had bought it to prepare for recording the narration of a film, *London*, which Paul was to read, as it is difficult to anticipate how one's words will sound when read by someone else, and the tape was extremely helpful. I have since often listened to it on long car journeys. The abridgement is very skilful, as they often are, and the story gains a degree of montage beyond that which characterises the original, for, as Eisenstein pointed out, Dickens was a pioneer of montage.

One of the strands omitted from the audiobook was the story of Caddy Jellyby's engagement and subsequent marriage to Prince Turveydrop, her dancing teacher, the fatally exploited son of old Mr Turveydrop, the proprietor of Turveydrop's Academy, a dancing school in Newman Street, in London, which is described as being 'in a sufficiently dingy house at the corner of an archway', and backs on to a mews. The only remaining archway in Newman Street is that above the entry to Newman Mews, which connects, via Newman Passage, a narrower archway adjacent to the Newman Arms, to Rathbone Street. On the north side of the Newman Street archway is a house which is perhaps not quite big enough to have contained Turveydrop's Academy, and is no longer dingy, being the premises of Cinecontact, where we were editing the film.

This encounter with its fictional past recalled a whole series of fateful associations with this corner of London, better known for its role in Michael Powell's *Peeping Tom*. A few doors along Rathbone Street are the former premises of the British Film Institute's now disbanded production division, where I spent months editing *London* with Larry Sider, with whom I was again working, and wrote the narration that had led me to acquire *Bleak House*. The first press interview prior to *London*'s release took place at a table outside the Newman Arms. Cinecontact's move to Newman Street had been the catalyst for the producer of my two previous films, who used to sub-let a corner of their previous office, to join Illuminations (whose office had once been in Newman Mews), the company for which we were making the film, which was how I ended up with two producers, which was why, eventually, I read *Bleak House*. The discovery of Mr Turveydrop's Academy, in the small hours of a sleepless January night, brought all this vividly to mind. *Bleak House* is set, approximately, in the 1830s. We finished editing the film in a room that looked onto the backs of some of the original houses in Rathbone Street, which now appeared, in a way they had never done before, to offer the possibility of contact with another time.

In the last 150 years or so, technology has radically altered the way we communicate, but the built environment has not changed anything like as much as people used to predict it would. The way we experience space now changes much faster than the fabric of the spaces that we occupy. When looking at images of the past, I have been increasingly struck by the contrast between the familiarity of the spaces depicted and our distance from the lives of those who then inhabited them. The ease with which we now communicate with distant spaces in the present may be a factor in this, but there is another reason, which is that the medium of film, too, has become old. The virtual past exists in many media – in the topography of novels, like *Bleak House*, in maps, paintings, photographs and so on – but film's duration, and its oneiric aspect, suggest analogies with consciousness, with lived experience. At the same time, film provokes seemingly unanswerable questions about the inner life of its human subjects in a way that the novel, for instance, does not – novelists enjoying access to the thoughts of their creations. Perhaps such questions *are* unanswerable, but perhaps, with the aid of literature and other sources, one can make the attempt. Time travel may not yet be an actual possibility, but it has long been a virtual one.

10

The City of the Future

At the beginning of the twentieth century, there seems to have been a relatively widespread expectation that new technologies and social structures would – or at least should – give rise to a radical transformation of urban space in the decades that were to follow. In retrospect, however, despite slum clearance in the 1930s, bombing during the Second World War, and the reconstruction and redevelopment that followed, city life has probably changed much more in other ways, often ways that involve people's perceptions. Technology has radically altered the way we communicate, but the technologies of building and construction have changed much less.

During the 1960s and early 1970s, in the UK and other older developed economies, the idea that widespread, large scale replacement of the built environment was necessary, desirable or possible lost most of whatever credibility it had previously had. Instead, it seems to be generally accepted that cities and other built landscapes typically evolve through only limited and gradual physical alteration. Rebuilding on a large scale now appears exceptional – the aftermath of disasters, war, or the sudden collapse of an industrial land use, as in the London docks.[1] The great majority of the UK's dwellings, for instance, are the first to have been built on the sites they occupy. Redevelopment was often traumatic, and with the increase in owner-occupation, both in the UK and elsewhere, the idea of replacing ageing, unsatisfactory housing has become difficult to contemplate.[2] Only about 70 per cent of urban land is residential, but the prospect of large-scale redevelopment is almost as unlikely for much non-residential urban space. Much of the new development that does occur today takes place on previously undeveloped or derelict land at the edges of or between existing settlements, and consists of only a narrow range of building types.[3]

During the 1920s, many avant-garde groups produced radical architectural proposals for future urban forms that influenced subsequent architectural production, but Surrealism was not among them. The first Surrealists devoted a great deal of attention to urban space and architecture, but none of them was an architect, and the movement does not seem to have attracted any architects until after the Second World War, when Frederick Kiesler aligned himself with Surrealism in New York and developed a polemic for 'magic architecture', now rather influential. Instead of producing designs for parts of Paris that called for the physical replacement of its fabric, the Surrealists' method of engaging with and arguably changing urban space was through subjective transformation. It was not necessary to design or build the Tour Saint-Jacques, for example, to include it in the canon of Surrealist architecture. It was enough to appropriate it, to declare its possession of hitherto overlooked (Surrealist) qualities.

This process of discovery, or rediscovery, of urban spaces closely resembles a now-familiar characteristic of the property markets of established cities. With increasing predictability, undervalued neighbourhoods are 'discovered' by artists and other creative types in search of cheap space, whose perception of aesthetic and other value becomes the basis for fashion, so that property values subsequently rise. Buildings attract new, more profitable uses, and hence sometimes refurbishment and alteration. Some buildings might even be replaced, but rarely with anything radically different, so that the general pattern of the city is not much altered, or is at least not much altered by altering the buildings. Since the 1970s, in much of the developed world, this kind of scenario has become popular with governments seeking strategies for urban regeneration.

Apart from the Surrealists, others have addressed the qualities of already-existing urban fabric more directly. In Chapter 10 of *The Death and Life of Great American Cities* (1961), Jane Jacobs wrote: 'Old ideas can sometimes use new buildings. New ideas must use old buildings.'[4] This statement was invoked by the recent UK government-appointed Urban Task Force, and is rarely questioned, although at least one of the assumptions behind it – that old buildings are cheaper to occupy than new buildings – probably no longer applies to anything like the extent that it did in the early 1960s. In London, the institutionalisation of Jacobs's insight is demonstrated by Tate Modern, the former power station that exemplifies the widely held preference of artists for working and exhibiting in spaces with a previous, often industrial use, which was explicitly referred to in the brief for the architectural competition for the design of its conversion. Inside Tate Modern, one finds aspects of this sensibility in works of art,[5] which perhaps also helped legitimise the idea that it would be possible to re-use the building successfully. Jacobs was writing in a context when neighbourhood renewal was still a frequent and grave threat to the well-being – even, as must have transpired more often than we will ever know, to the life-expectancy – of inhabitants of inner-city neighbourhoods. Since her book was first published, the redevelopment of large areas of existing cities has become rare, and it has become much more difficult to demolish buildings. This is partly due to the change in culture that her book signalled, and to another attitude that is not so much innate conservatism as an understandable belief that any replacement structure is likely to be even more architecturally impoverished than its predecessor.

A more recent phenomenon, particularly in the UK, has been the revival of the Situationist idea of psychogeography. This, and the *dérive*, were techniques to explore and extend the imaginative, experiential qualities of urban and other landscapes, as part of a wider attempt to achieve a revolutionary transformation of everyday life. As such, it continued the efforts of the Surrealists, but the Situationist group did include architects and others who produced radical architectural proposals to which psychogeography and so on were seen, at least by some, as preliminary. In 1990s London, however, psychogeography seems to have been an end in itself, and as such to have lost much of this character and purpose. Instead of avant-garde architecture, we have the *Time Out Book of London Walks*.

A similar 'procedure of everyday creativity' was identified more positively by Michel de Certeau who wrote, as long ago as 1974, in the introduction to his *The Practice of Everyday Life*:

> Increasingly constrained, yet less and less concerned with these vast frameworks, the individual detaches himself from them without being able to escape them and can henceforth only try to outwit them, to pull tricks on them, to rediscover, within an electronicized and computerized megalopolis, the 'art' of the hunters and rural folk of earlier days . . .
>
>   Witold Gombrowicz, an acute visionary, gave this politics its hero . . . whose refrain is 'when one does not have what one wants, one must want what one has'.[6]

De Certeau emphasises the positive side to this, comparing it to 'the ambiguity that subverted from within the Spanish colonizers' "success" in imposing their own culture on the indigenous Indians', but Gombrowicz's character's motto is a reminder of how tactless it would be today to retain any expectation of everyday experience of utopian, revolutionary, 'magic' or even *progressive* architecture. Progressive architecture is still produced by, and to some extent for, an international élite, but in circumstances that increasingly resemble those of a reservation (from market forces, 'philistinism' and so on) protected by a cultural establishment. New housing architecture, for example, has not been produced on any scale in the UK for decades, since the elimination of the public-sector housing programme. Most present-day predictions of the spaces of the 'city of the future' are found in fiction (often in the cinema), where they are largely dystopian. In any case, were anyone now to attempt to envisage a radically improved future, it is unlikely that it would be formulated as an architectural proposal.

Instead, in the UK and elsewhere, cities might now be distinguished not so much by the merits of their spatial form, their society, culture and so on, but by how successfully they negotiate continual social, economic and technological change. This often seems to involve finding ways of getting the best out of predicaments characterised by opposition or conflict, such as that already mentioned between the relative merits of old and new buildings. One might compose a list of similar oppositions, which would include those between art and architecture;[7] between creativity and domesticity (between thinking and dwelling);[8] between centralisation and decentralisation; between globalised finance and globalised production[9] – and many others, not least of which would be that between wealth and poverty. One wonders whether, perhaps, old buildings, art, creativity, centralisation, globalised finance and wealth might have something in common, as might new buildings, architecture, domesticity, decentralisation, globalised production and poverty. If such a distinction is at least partly valid, it might be further examined in terms of an underlying shift in the balance between virtuality and materiality over the last hundred years or so.

The decades either side of 1900 were a period of rapid technological and other changes, many of which involved the perception of space. It is estimated that between 1816 and 1915, as many as 52 million emigrants left Europe for overseas destinations, more than half of them for the United States, the largest numbers leaving after about 1880.[10] Among new technologies, the first 'standard layout' car was produced in 1891, and the first projected films exhibited in 1895. The coincidence of cinema and emigration is particularly intriguing when one considers how much of cinema came from the major destination of emigrants, and that both might be seen to offer the possibility of a 'new' or other world. The skyscraper, electrically lit and artificially ventilated, also dates from the turn of the century, arguably from Burnham and Root's Reliance Building in Chicago, of 1895. Transatlantic radio communication was first achieved in 1902, and powered flight in 1903. The first deep electric underground railway[11] opened in 1890, and the electric tram,[12] the incandescent electric lamp, the telephone and the phonograph were all establishing themselves during the period. Ocean-going steamships became much bigger: from Cunard's *Campania*, at 12,950 tonnes the biggest in 1893, to the Hamburg-Amerika *Vaterland*, 54,282 tonnes in 1914.

Imaginary or virtual space was familiar in the nineteenth century as the space of the novel – 'Dickens's London', for instance – or as the spaces of photography, painting and so on; but with moving pictures, new communications technology, mass emigration and cheaper travel, virtual space became much more pervasive. The invention of cinematography began an evolution of 'animated photographs' which includes silent and sound cinema, television, and the vast proliferation of other electronic moving images that continues today. Moving pictures combined the likeness of the photograph with the duration of consciousness and narrative, offering the possibility of a simulated experience of movement through space, as in the 'phantom rides' that were a popular subject of early films.[13]

During the century since, mechanisation and subsequently automation have radically transformed the availability, production and distribution of material things like food, consumer goods and other mass-produced items, especially since the widespread application of computers during the last three decades. As a result, though construction has been mechanised to a limited extent, the cost of building has increased enormously compared with that of most other artefacts, and has probably also increased when compared with average earnings, so that building has become more expensive.[14] For this and other reasons (planning constraints, for instance) the production and maintenance of built space is now a good deal more difficult than it was a century ago.

The results of both these trends are very visible, especially in the UK, as if the increased relative cost of building and the proliferation of virtual space, and of economic activity that takes place in or via virtual space, have disadvantaged the visible landscape. Although people in the UK are, on average, far better off than their predecessors of a hundred years ago, and are much better housed, the built environment is characterised by high levels of dilapidation,

IBM Customer Education Centre

"...and if the Minister rings, explain that I'm at school this week."

At a very special school. On a course where every new boy is a leader. . But a leader who knows the value of refreshing his leadership in today's terms; and tomorrow's.

The IBM Directors' Computer Concept Course is carefully designed to help top executives of IBM's British customers to get the most out of their computer investment. It takes one working week. It is run by some of the world's most able computer instructors—men whose own training is distilled from the unrivalled pool of

IBM's multi-national knowledge and experience. It doesn't blind with science. It simplifies, clarifies, communicates. It answers the many questions which top decision-makers ask. Many questions which all boil down to one: how do I make the most effective, most profitable use of my IBM data processing equipment?

Executives without ministerial access are welcome too—on this and a vast range of other computer appreciation courses. And for specialists—data processing managers present and

future, programmers, analysts—IBM provides detailed, intensive, highly sophisticated instruction.

Some 5,000 men and women each year take more than 500 different courses on 50 different subjects. Thus IBM ensures that all its customers know what they need to know, to play their part in the proper handling of their IBM equipment.

At IBM our responsibility to the customer begins long before we install a computer.

IBM

IBM United Kingdom Limited, 101, Wigmore Street, London, W.1. Telephone: Welbeck 6600

IBM advertisement, *Weekend Telegraph*, 27 May 1966

poor maintenance and new buildings of a far lower quality than the alleged success of the UK's economy might lead one to expect. Even inadequate property is often very expensive, as is seen in the housing market and elsewhere, as in the UK's curiously overpriced, poor-quality hotels. The building industry is perceived as an unattractive career choice, so that building skills are in short supply. There are official attempts to address the perceived inadequacies of the UK's building industry,[15] but so far without widespread success. In less deregulated, more social-democratic economies in Europe, the standard of the built environment is much higher, but the pressures are the same.

The predicament of building in advanced economies does seem to be relatively recent, dating from the early twentieth century. For example, considered as an artefact, the English vernacular house appears to have reached a kind of peak in the arts-and-crafts-influenced examples of the years between 1900 and the First World War. These houses were often more conscientiously put together than their Victorian predecessors, with improvements such as damp courses, but they were built by building tradesmen whose wages improved after the First World War,[16] so that new middle-class houses became more expensive and less sophisticated, a trend that continues today. The predicament of surviving late Victorian and Edwardian public buildings – art galleries, museums, town halls and so on – suggests a similar subsequent decline in the affordability of building since the years before the First World War.

A similar phenomenon is visible in central London. A balloon view of the area between the Strand and Battersea in 1851 shows a city with a physical form that has changed quite significantly since. In 1851, the pleasure gardens at Vauxhall still survived, and the expanse of elevated track that now dominates the landscape south of the river between Battersea and Waterloo Station was still comparatively narrow. On the opposite bank of the river stood the enormous Millbank Penitentiary. Brunel's Hungerford suspension bridge connected the south bank to Hungerford Market, the future site of Charing Cross Station. At the north-east corner of Oxford Street and Tottenham Court Road, there was a brewery.

Balloon view of London seen from Hampstead, 1851 (detail)

During the following decades, the railways extended to Charing Cross and Victoria Stations; the Victoria and Albert embankments were built, and the construction of Admiralty Arch, Charing Cross Road, Shaftesbury Avenue, Kingsway and the Aldwych all involved large-scale replacement of the previous fabric. By about 1910, however, this part of the city was recognisably the space it is today. Individual buildings have since been replaced (some with replicas), but it would appear that, at least in this part of London, a degree of stasis set in. Even in the City of London, where replacement of individual buildings is a continual process, the general form – the street layout, the scale of most of the buildings – is not *radically* different from that of circa 1910. London is much bigger than it was in 1910, but most of the fabric that existed then has not changed anything like as much as might have been expected early in the twentieth century. Much of inner London's housing stock is older than that of other UK and European cities, so that many Londoners spend most of their time in spaces built and formerly inhabited by previous generations, and psychogeography, and Gombrowicz's irony, suit the predicament of London very well.

Although the onset of this relative stasis in city space, such as it is, appears to date from the period of early moving pictures, it seems unlikely that there is any very direct connection (as there might be with, for example, the survival and recycling of fashions in clothing). The proliferation of moving pictures is only one of many elements in a much wider technological and economic evolution that might have disadvantaged building. In any case, during the last few decades, moving pictures themselves have been subjected to exactly the same kind of pressure as urban space. The spread of electronic image formats has pushed up the relative cost of photochemically originated films distributed as 35mm prints; years of low-resolution video have softened up audiences' expectations of picture quality; computer games and so on compete for cinema audiences' spending; budgets rise, and cinemas themselves, empty or nearly empty for most of the day, appear increasingly unprofitable as real estate. On the other hand, the representation of urban space in films does seem to be a factor in the current scenarios of urban regeneration. Popular cinema is a conservative industry, so films are rarely a vehicle for the initial artistic 'rediscovery' of a place, but the sight of a familiar space in a film can momentarily banish the sense of marginality that haunts even the most central urban locations. This transformation is enabled by the combination of fiction and *photogénie* that characterises a successful film, and is very like the attraction that led audiences to queue up to see themselves on screen in the factory-gate and other local films that were exhibited at fairgrounds all over the north of England in the 1900s.

The Surrealist sensitivity to urban space is perhaps most explicit in Louis Aragon's *Le Paysan de Paris*, first published in 1926, the book to which Walter Benjamin refers as having inspired his *Paris, Capital of the Nineteenth Century*. Aragon's first published writing, however, was the essay 'On *Décor*', which appeared in September 1918 in Louis Delluc's *Le Film*, in which he wrote:

> To endow with a poetic value that which does not yet possess it, to wilfully restrict the field of vision so as to intensify expression: these are two properties that help make cinematic *décor* the adequate setting of modern beauty.[17]

The desire for a poetic experience of ordinary, everyday phenomena was central to Surrealism and many other strands of modernism, from Baudelaire or even De Quincey onwards, but it was perhaps most readily achieved through photography and cinematography. It seems quite possible, therefore, that it was Aragon's experience of the cinema – as he describes it in 'On *Décor*' – that led him to the Surrealist sensitivity to actual everyday surroundings explored in *Le Paysan de Paris*, a sensibility recalled by present-day writers' and artists' treatments of already-existing urban spaces.

During the 1970s, the film–architecture relationship became a fashionable subject in architectural discourse. It seemed odd that it should have taken architects so long to develop a theoretical interest in cinema, but previous attempts were probably frustrated by the relative inaccessibility of film space as a research subject before the introduction of the video recorder. Critically significant architects such as Jean Nouvel and Bernard Tschumi have produced buildings informed by their readings of cinematic space, which seem to draw mainly on the idea of cinematic montage. In these, film space was considered as a model for architectural space, but more recently much of the discussion of film in architectural circles appears to have declined into an exploration of influences that the imageries of architecture and cinema exert on one another. The spaces of cinema are among those that Henri Lefebvre identifies as *representational* spaces,[18] and representational spaces exert an influence on architecture, but cinema is only one of many such sources among which literature, for instance, might be thought at least as important. The imagery of architecture, inevitably, influences the look of films, and the imagery of cinema might influence the look of architecture, though probably rather less than has sometimes been suggested; but such observations seem to miss the point, which is that what distinguishes film space more than anything else is the extent to which it is very *unlike* actual space as we experience it.

In *The Production of Space*, Lefebvre writes:

> The idea of a new life is at once realistic and illusory – and hence neither true nor false. What is true is that the preconditions for a different life have already been created, and that that other life is thus on the cards. What is false is the assumption that being on the cards and being imminent are the same thing, that what is immediately possible is necessarily a world away from what is only a distant possibility, or even an impossibility. The fact is that the space which contains the realized preconditions of another life is the same one as prohibits what those preconditions make possible.

In the spaces of cinema, 'the realized preconditions of another life' are made visible and, within the film, permanent. In everyday life, they might be glimpsed, but ultimately remain ephemeral.

Lefebvre continues:

> The seeming limpidity of that space is therefore a delusion: it appears to make elucidation unnecessary, but in reality it urgently

requires elucidation. A total revolution – material, economic, social, political, psychic, cultural, erotic, etc. – seems to be in the offing, as though already immanent to the present. To change life, however, we must first change space.[19]

It seems unlikely that Lefebvre intended this statement to be read as a polemic for a radical physical transformation of the built environment but, equally, he is not referring to space merely as it is socially and politically constructed. A longed-for social reconstruction of already-existing spaces, however emancipating, would not overcome their physical shortcomings. Cinematic reconstruction of everyday space might suggest the possibility of its social and political reconstruction,[20] but the materiality of architectural space remains, and appears increasingly problematic.

In Part III of his *Modern Architecture: A Critical History*, published in 1980, Kenneth Frampton quotes Shadrach Woods, co-architect of the Free University in Berlin, writing in 1967:

> What are we waiting for? To read the news about a new armed attack with even more esoteric weapons, news which comes to us through the air captured by our marvellous transistorized instruments somewhere deep in our more and more savaged dwellings? Our weapons become more sophisticated; our houses more and more brutish. Is that the balance sheet for the richest civilisation since time began?

Frampton follows this with another quotation, from Giancarlo de Carlo's *Legitimizing Architecture* of 1968, which includes:

> At the same time, we have a right to ask 'why' housing should be as cheap as possible and not, for example, rather expensive; 'why' instead of making every effort to reduce it to minimum levels of surface, of thickness, of materials, we should not try to make it spacious, protected, isolated, comfortable, well equipped, rich in opportunities for privacy, communication, exchange, personal creativity. No one, in fact, can be satisfied by an answer which appeals

to the scarcity of available resources, when we all know how much
is spent on wars, on the construction of missiles and anti-ballistic
systems, on moon projects, on research for the defoliation of
forests inhabited by partisans and for the paralyzation of the
demonstrators emerging from the ghettos, on hidden persuasion,
on the invention of artificial needs, etc.[21]

In the decades since, 'marvellous transistorized instruments' and
similar devices have continued to proliferate. In advanced economies, reductions in the cost of consumer items, air travel and so on
might suggest that nearly everyone has become wealthier since the
late 1960s, but it is not difficult to argue otherwise. In 1997, a study
by the UK's New Economics Foundation concluded that an index
of sustainable economic welfare in the UK had risen from 1950
until the mid 1970s, but between 1976 and 1996 had declined by 25
per cent, despite an increase in GDP per capita of 44 per cent.[22]
Increases in consumption had been offset by environmental
damage, increased inequality and other factors.

In retrospect, the 1970s appear increasingly intriguing, not least
as the period during which computers and similar technology first
became widespread for large-scale applications in industry and
administration, and the personal computer was developed.
Although often characterised as a decade of failure, economic stagnation and the slide into neoliberalism, in which the emancipatory
promises of the 1960s signally failed to materialise, the 1970s were
the period in which many aspects of our present economic reality
were first put in place.[23] We live now in a future, not as it was imagined in the 1960s, but as it was actually constructed during the
1970s. The early 1970s are also the period most often associated
with the 'shift in the structure of feeling' that separates modernity
from postmodernity, since when the coherent imagination of alternative 'better' futures has largely disappeared, so that while we
might see ourselves living in a version of a previous period's future,
we have no such imagined future of our own.[24]

The late 1960s and early 1970s were a relatively successful period
for films made in the UK, so one might look in some of these for

evidence of what, if anything, has changed. In the spaces of Michelangelo Antonioni's *Blow-Up* (1966), Joseph Losey's *Accident* (1967), Lindsay Anderson's *If . . . .* (1968), Donald Cammell and Nicolas Roeg's *Performance* (1970) or even Stanley Kubrick's *A Clockwork Orange* (1971), there is a definite sense of the materiality of the period, which does seem rather luxurious when compared with that of today's landscapes and artefacts, however abundant these may be. In *If . . . .*, for example, roads near Cheltenham are lined with enormous elm trees, long gone, and the town centre seems in much better physical condition than it is today, though the citizens of today's Cheltenham are almost certainly more prosperous. It also seems extremely odd (in the era of penny-pinching private-sector prisons) that Kubrick should have imagined a near future in which a correctional facility might be represented by the pristine spaces of the nearly new Brunel University. Much of this feeling of material quality can be put down to the skills of cinematographers and art directors (and the manufacturers of filmstock), though these too have become scarce. An everyday landscape of 35mm cine colour images made by outstanding cinematographers[25] compares very favourably with today's space routinely represented in indifferent electronic imagery. Nonetheless, the experience offered by these and other films is extremely valuable. Moving pictures offer a number of possibilities to architecture – in representing spaces that do not yet exist, or as a model for new architecture and architectural theory – but as the medium ages, one wonders if perhaps it offers most as an approach to experiencing the spaces of other times. Architecture is increasingly seen as a process structured in time. In films, one can explore the spaces of the past, in order to better anticipate the spaces of the future.

11

Film as Spatial Critique

Before films were distributed on video, it was difficult to explore their spaces unless one had access to specialised equipment – an 'analytical' projector or an editing table. The continual and often rapid succession of images that generally constitutes the experience of watching a film is not very conducive to accurate recollection, especially of anything peripheral to a narrative, and it is difficult to draw or make notes in the darkness of a cinema. Perhaps this is why, with a few significant exceptions, architects' theoretical engagement with film was delayed until recent decades. With the introduction of domestic video recorders, and the refinement of the possibility to pause and search, cinema became more accessible for architectural exploration.[1]

Since the 1970s, architects have explored cinema as a source of spatial concepts applicable to architecture, but the excitement that accompanied this discovery seems to have passed. In retrospect, it seems to me – as an architect diverted into making films – that film has a more general significance for architecture as a means of developing a critique, temporal and otherwise, of actual architectural and urban space. What initially attracted – and continues to attract – me to the medium is that it offers the possibility, albeit constrained, to experience non-existent spaces, and in particular to experience spatial qualities seldom, not yet, or no longer encountered in ordinary experience. These spaces may be non-existent either because they have not yet been produced, or because they no longer exist.

'Spaces that have not yet been produced' might exist physically, but not experientially or socially, while 'spaces that no longer exist' may still exist physically, but not socially, or they may no longer exist at all. Films can represent physically imaginary spaces, or proposals for spaces to be realised in the future, but for me the medium's allure has always derived from its capacity to imaginatively transform already-existing space, and from the possibility it offers to experience spaces of the past to somewhat similar effect.

I would like to suggest that film space can offer an implicit critique of actual space, so that looking at and researching films can constitute a kind of architectural criticism. I would also suggest that one can make films (and I suppose I would claim to have done so) that set out to criticise architectural space rather than simply depict it (which, given the marked differences between film space and actual architecture, is much more difficult). Lastly, I would suggest that film[2] from the past that depicts urban and other architectural space of its time can offer an implicit critique of similar spaces of the present, and can inform our understanding of the ways in which urban and other landscapes change in time.

A few years ago I embarked on a project to explore urban space as it appears in films made before the mid 1900s.[3] The following

Carrington Street, Nottingham in 2003, with inset from *Tram Rides Through Nottingham, Carrington Street,* Mitchell and Kenyon (1902)

paragraphs set out the context for this exploration, and identify coincident periods of transition in the histories of architecture, urban space and film.

Until the mid 1900s, most films were between one and three minutes long, and consisted of one or very few unedited takes. The Lumière company's films, for example, are typically from 48 to 52 feet long, and last about a minute. They were made by exposing a complete roll of film, often without stopping. Most early films were actualities, not fiction, and many were street scenes or views of other topographical subjects, some of them photographed from moving vehicles and boats. Cinematographers would sometimes pause if there was a lull in the ambient action, or if the view was blocked, but other kinds of editing are unusual. The reconstruction of time and space by joining individual shots together was an aspect of film-making that began to dominate only after about 1907.

Tom Gunning has called this early cinema 'the cinema of attractions',[4] a reference to Eisenstein's 'montage of attractions', conceived as a new model for theatre. Eisenstein took the term from the fairground, where his favourite attraction was the roller coaster, the Russian for which translates as 'the American Mountains'. There is an early Biograph film *A Ride on a Switchback* (1900, or possibly 1898), which was made by mounting a camera not on a roller coaster, as early films sometimes were, but on a railway engine. A switchback was a railway engineers' device for negotiating steep gradients with a siding and a set of points, entering by one branch and backing out into the other, so as to avoid the construction of a hairpin bend. Biograph's film was photographed in mountains near Fort Lee, New Jersey, which one might imagine were *the* (or at least some) American Mountains. Films photographed from the front of railway engines were known as 'phantom rides', presumably because of the sensation of disembodied consciousness they offer. Views from other moving vehicles – trams and, later, cars – are sometimes called phantom rides, but the term seems to have been most specific to the view from the front of a locomotive, which was then seldom encountered in ordinary experience, even by an engine driver.

As Gunning writes, after 1907 'the cinema of attractions does not disappear with the dominance of narrative, but rather goes underground, both into certain avant-garde practices and as a component of narrative films'.[5] There is a story that Andy Warhol's *Kiss* (1963) was prompted by an archive viewing of Edison's *Kiss of May Irvin and John C. Rice* (1896), and whether or not it was, the formal evolution of Warhol's films – from the hundred-foot rolls of *Sleep* (1963) and *Kiss* (1963) to the 1,200-foot rolls of the two-screen *The Chelsea Girls* (1966) – strikingly resembles that of early film.[6] In narrative cinema, phantom rides appear in *films noirs*, often at the beginning of a film or in title sequences, as in Fritz Lang's *Human Desire* (1954), Mike Hodges's *Get Carter* (1971), and the car shots in Jacques Tourneur's *Out of the Past* (1947), Edgar G. Ulmer's *Detour* (1945) – looking backwards – and Robert Aldrich's *Kiss Me Deadly* (1955). Since the 1960s the cinema of attractions has emerged from underground, in films and installations by a wide variety of artists and other film-makers, most of them outside the mainstream of Western cinema. Whether in the gallery or in what used to be called art cinema, there is a tendency towards some of the forms of early film.

Both early films and these more recent examples differ from what became the dominant form in the way they represent space on a screen. In films constructed as montage, space is assembled in time, as an implied continuity of fragments. In most early films, space is represented within a single frame, either static or moving. Early films are also less likely to direct the viewer's attention to a single subject in the frame: one's eye can more easily wander in their spaces, and because of this they invite (or even require) repeated viewing. Moving-camera films often create a striking illusion of three-dimensionality, which early film-makers sometimes referred to explicitly as 'the stereoscopic effect'.

Between the mid 1900s and the outbreak of the First World War, the spaces and spatial experiences characteristic of industrialised economies appear to have undergone significant transformation. These transitions have been described in a variety of ways: for example, in his afterword to the English translation of Henri

Courtesy of the British Film Institute

Lister Gate, Nottingham in 2003, with inset from *Tram Rides Through Nottingham, Lister Gate*, Mitchell and Kenyon (1902)

Lefebvre's definitive *La Production de l'espace*, first published in 1974, but in English only in 1991, the geographer David Harvey quoted a passage in Lefebvre's opening chapter:

> The fact is that around 1910 a certain space was shattered. It was the space of common sense, of knowledge (*savoir*), of social practice, of political power, a space thitherto enshrined in everyday discourse, just as in abstract thought, as the environment of and channel for communications; the space, too, of classical perspective and geometry, developed from the Renaissance onwards on the basis of the Greek tradition (Euclid, logic) and bodied forth in Western art and philosophy, as in the form of the city and the town . . . Euclidean and perspectivist space have disappeared as systems of reference, along with other former 'commonplaces' such as the town, history, paternity, the tonal system in music, traditional morality, and so forth. This was truly a crucial moment.[7]

Harvey had already quoted from this passage in his *The Condition of Postmodernity* (1990), following mention of 'the incredible confusions and oppositions across a spectrum of possible reactions to the growing sense of crisis in the experience of time and space, that had been gathering since 1848 and seemed to come to a head just before the First World War', and noted 'that 1910–14 is roughly the period that many historians of modernism (beginning with Virginia Woolf and D. H. Lawrence) point to as crucial in the evolution of modernist thinking'.[8]

For Harvey, the crisis was one 'of technological innovation, of capitalist dynamics across space [and] cultural production'. He notes the slightly different emphasis of Stephen Kern who, in *The Culture of Time and Space 1880–1918* (1983), offered 'generalizations about the essential cultural developments of the period'.[9] Other writers have dealt with these in detail: for John Berger, 'The Moment of Cubism' was the period between 1907 and 1914, and during the period 1900–14 'the developments which converged at the beginning of the twentieth century in Europe changed the meaning of time and space'.[10] Berger listed these as:

> An interlocking world system of imperialism; opposed to it, a socialist international; the founding of modern physics, physiology and sociology; the increasing use of electricity, the invention of radio and the cinema; the beginnings of mass production; the publishing of mass-circulation newspapers; the new structural possibilities offered by the availability of steel and aluminium; the rapid development of the chemical industries and the production of synthetic materials; the appearance of the motor car and the aeroplane.[11]

More recent writing (including that of Kern and Harvey) has stressed the role of telecommunications; others mention emigration, both within and away from Europe.[12] Some of these developments suggest comparisons with the present.

At about the same time, architectural theorists began to develop new concepts of architectural space. For Reyner Banham, in *Theory and Design in the First Machine Age* (1960), 'a series of revolutionary gestures around 1910, largely connected with the Cubist and Futurist movements, were the main point of departure for the development of Modern architecture'.[13] Banham's narrative is that of evolving concepts of space, specifically 'the change-over from the Lippsian idea of space, as *felt volume* [my emphasis] . . . to the later concept of space as a three-dimensional continuum, capable of metrical subdivision, without sacrifice of its continuity'.[14] The idea of space as volume enclosed by solid surfaces (characteristic of early modern architects such as Voysey or Berlage, and of Cerdà's Barcelona) began to give way to concepts in which the solidity of matter was less certain, just as the early modernist city, with its bicycles and electric trams, would give way to the city of the motor car. By 1929 László Moholy-Nagy was able to formulate the minimum definition – 'space is the relation between the position of bodies'[15] – which for Banham confirmed 'the whole revolution in architectural theory that had been going on since 1908'.[16] One of Moholy-Nagy's earlier spatial expositions was his 1921–22 proposal for a film, *Dynamic of the Metropolis*, which somewhat anticipates Dziga Vertov's 1929 *Man with a Movie Camera*. *Dynamic of the Metropolis* was never realised, but by 1929 Moholy-Nagy had made *Berliner Stilleben* (1926) and perhaps also *Marseille, Vieux-Port* (1929), so that the 'minimum definition' of modernist space was put forward by a theorist who was also an experienced film-maker.

Banham saw the distinction between Theodor Lipps's and Moholy-Nagy's spatial concepts as sequential, but the idea of space as 'felt volume' only slightly pre-dated the subsequent, more abstract formulation – it appears that the word 'space' (*raum*) was not used in Lipps's (or any other architectural) sense before about 1900[17] – and Lipps's concept never really went away. The distinction between the two spatial concepts is very like that between Gunning's two kinds of cinema, and the spatiality of the early films – their depiction of architectural space within a single frame, their uninterrupted, lengthy spatio-temporal continuities (the tram rides especially) and the 'stereoscopic effect' – is easy to identify with Lipps's formulation. Banham's *Theory and Design* was published in 1960, before the revival of urbanism in architectural theory in the

mid 1970s, since when architects and others have attempted to
revive this early modernist space, just as film-makers have revived
some of the forms of early cinema. Both Lipps's space and the
'cinema of attractions' might be seen as early modernist forms
which were eclipsed in the late 1900s, as part of a wider cultural
transformation, but have since re-emerged, usually in opposition to
the mainstream architectures and cinemas of Western and other
capitalist cultures.

In *The Condition of Postmodernity*, Harvey also quoted the famous
passage from Walter Benjamin's 'The Work of Art in the Age of
Mechanical Reproduction' (1936):

> Our taverns and our metropolitan streets, our offices and furnished
> rooms, our railroad stations and our factories appeared to have us
> locked up hopelessly. Then came the film and burst this prison-
> world asunder by the dynamite of the tenth of a second, so that
> now, in the midst of its far-flung ruins and debris, we calmly and
> adventurously go travelling.[18]

Benjamin's 'now' refers to film as it had evolved after the mid 1900s
– his essay, published in 1936, mentions nothing earlier than the
films of Abel Gance, Vertov and Joris Ivens – but it is not entirely
clear at what date 'came the film and burst this prison-world asunder'. If the development of cinema was a significant factor in the
transformation of urban and other space during the 1900s, one
wonders whether this was the development of cinema per se, or
the development of cinema with editing, narrative and close-up as
it was undertaken after the middle of the decade. The fragmentation Benjamin describes can be identified in post-1910 experience
as a breaking up of space into individual shots, in which case 'the
dynamite of the tenth of a second' is the interval between the end
of one shot and the beginning of the next, rather than the medium's primary fragmentation of continuous duration into the
discontinuous individual frames of a single shot. But the essay also
famously stresses 'the incomparable significance of Atget, who,
around 1900, took photographs of deserted Paris streets',[19] and it

might seem to us (over seventy years later) that in some ways one could 'calmly and adventurously go travelling' (even) more easily in the early 1900s than in the period of Gance and Vertov.

Whatever the date of the films that Benjamin had in mind, something happened to the medium in the mid 1900s. The change that Gunning identified seems to have followed a distinct lull in output, during or soon after which many of the pioneers ceased production. After the mid 1900s, films are generally longer but with shorter shots, close-ups and, increasingly, fiction and studio sets; few of them show very much of ordinary landscapes. When they do, the shots are usually so short as to permit relatively little exploration, even when examined frame-by-frame. In contrast, the brief, continuous or near-continuous films of spatial subjects made by the Lumière and Biograph companies and their contemporaries before about 1903 accumulate an extensive document of ordinary, everyday spaces of their period: the spaces that Lefebvre and others suggest were radically transformed soon afterwards. In enabling us to see so much of this landscape, these early films are truly extraordinary, as they offer the most extensive views of the landscape of another time at or just before the moment of that landscape's transformation – a transformation brought about (at least in part) by the development of the very medium in which the opportunity to explore these long-lost spaces was constructed.

What do these films mean for us? On looking at them, what struck me first was a contrast between their often familiar-looking landscapes and the unfamiliarity of the society glimpsed in them. In the last hundred years, the material and other circumstances of the UK's population have altered enormously,[20] but much of the urban fabric of the 1900s survives, often – like so much of the built environment – in a surprisingly dilapidated condition. In terms of life expectancy, physical health, income, mobility and so on, we are far better off than our predecessors of a hundred years ago: developed economies experience unprecedented levels of consumption and GDP per head, but in other respects – especially when measured in terms of social, cultural and environmental assets – wealth has not increased anything like as much. In some

ways, in some places, it has probably decreased.[21] In emphasising
this, the films might be thought subversive.

Walking in the streets of UK towns and cities today, the decline
of what Lefebvre described as 'the environment of and channel
for communications . . . in the form of the city and the town' is
easily recognised. One often detects a sense of absence, even in
the centre of London. The spatial qualities suggested by many
early films are very like some of those that attract tourists to less
advanced or (some) socialist economies – to places where arti-
sanal production or its past products survive, where domesticity
is still found in city centres, and where there are fewer cars, or at
least less traffic engineering. In advanced economies, such environmental qualities are typically achieved or retained through
socialist (as in, say, Barcelona) or social-democratic (as in the
Netherlands) politics.

In this context, Lefebvre's shattered 'space of common sense'
suggests both the spatial concepts of Lipps and the urban design
of Camillo Sitte. In 1903, Lipps 'argued that our bodies uncon-
sciously empathised with architectural form',[22] and Sitte,

> rooted in the craftworker tradition of late nineteenth-century
> Vienna . . . sought to construct spaces that would make the city's
> people 'secure and happy' . . . He therefore set out to create . . .
> spaces – plazas and squares – that would promote the preservation
> and even re-creation of a sense of community.[23]

Such ideas re-emerged in the postmodern urbanism of the 1970s,
for which early films might initially seem to offer some support,
with their depiction of what to us appear 'traditional' urban spaces
in which we might imagine we could be 'secure and happy', spaces
which 'would promote the preservation and even re-creation of a
sense of community'. Sitte's polemic, however, was not in favour
of the actually-existing spaces of the 1900s – the spaces that appear
in the films – but against them, 'abhorring the narrow and technical
functionalism that seemed to attach to the lust for commercial
profit', and seeking 'to overcome fragmentation and provide a

"community life-outlook'",[24] rather as we might today. Also, though Sitte is popular with present-day urban designers, his desire for spaces that he believed would promote 'community' was not unproblematic. As Harvey writes:

> many of the Viennese artisans whom Sitte championed . . . were later to mass in the squares, piazzas and living spaces that Sitte wanted to create, in order to express their virulent opposition to internationalism, turning to anti-semitism . . . and the place-specific myths of Nazism.[25]

The spaces of UK cities in the early 1900s were subject to transformations at least as sudden as any we experience today,[26] but there were few cars until later in the decade.[27] Early films depict a space in which there are electricity and telecommunications, but not much oil, so that the transformations of circa 1910 can be seen in terms of the coming of the oil economy and the motor car, which since the mid 1970s has been so widely cast in opposition to conventional formulations of *dwelling*, and to certain kinds of urban space and architecture. Here again, pre-1907 films might seem to offer a polemic – for streets without cars, for architecture, for public transport, and for a less centralised, less dematerialised economy. They might even resemble science fiction: a future in which the costs of distant labour, and of energy, and hence transport, have increased, so that production becomes more local. At the same time, we can assume that, as images, the films bestow an illusory coherence on their subjects. The spaces that appear in the films were dynamic, subject to tensions as unsettling as (and sometimes surprisingly similar to) any we experience today.

12

Phantom Rides:
The Railway and Early Film

In his history of the panorama, Stephan Oetterman quotes a report that, in 1834, a panorama of the railway between Liverpool and Manchester was exhibited in Brooklyn, having been previously exhibited in England. The Liverpool and Manchester Railway, generally regarded as the first regular city-to-city passenger railway service, had opened in 1830. Oetterman writes that panoramas simulating movement through landscape became popular in the English-speaking countries from the 1820s, suggesting that 'the moving panorama anticipated, in art, the speed of travel which the railroads would soon make a reality'. He notes a connection with migration, and that the panorama 'proved highly successful . . . in motivating prospective settlers to consider California'.[1]

Moving or extended panoramas were popular in Britain, as well as in the United States, where the static panorama seems not to have caught on to the extent that it did in Europe. Views of landscape painted on lengths of canvas were rolled between two cylinders, one on each side of a stage or similar field of view, so that the landscape appeared to pass by, as if the audience were travelling in a vehicle or on a boat. A *Grand Panorama of a Whaling Voyage Round the World* was first exhibited in New Bedford in 1848.[2] In the same year, Charles Dickens described the exhibition in London of *Banvard's Geographical Panorama of the Mississippi and Missouri Rivers* at the Egyptian Hall, Piccadilly. Banvard's panorama depicted a journey of 1,200 miles, was claimed in its early publicity to be three miles long, and took two hours to pass before the audience.[3] Wolfgang Schivelbusch notes that the decline of the panorama coincides with the growth of the rail-way;[4] but the panorama enjoyed a second popularity after about 1880, and moving panoramas were still being produced as late as 1900, when a *Trans-Siberian Express* was exhibited in the Paris *Universal Exposition*.[5]

Moving panoramas were more portable and perhaps easier to reduce in scale than static 360-degree panoramas, which were conventionally exhibited in purpose-built rotundas. In the famous sequence in Max Ophüls's *Letter from an Unknown Woman* (1948), set in Vienna in 'about 1900', the characters played by Joan Fontaine and Louis Jourdan visit the Prater, its Riesenrad (erected in 1897) in the background, where they linger in a fairground panorama fitted out as a compartment of a railway carriage, past the window of which endless but rather soon repeated views of landscapes – Venice, Switzerland – are moved by pedal power. 'We have no more countries' says the operator after a while. 'Then we'll begin again,' says Jourdan, 'we'll revisit the scenes of our youth'. This scene, in which the mechanism is very clearly demonstrated, is not part of Stefan Zweig's original story.[6]

Both cinema and the railway offer more or less predetermined and repeatable spatio-temporal continuities, so that it is perhaps not surprising that railways crop up in cinema as often as they do. Films even physically resemble railway tracks – long, parallel-sided strips divided laterally by frame lines and perforations, as is the railway by sleepers. Cinema is one of the technologies that devel-oped during the period of rapid globalisation between 1880 and 1918, and is associated with electrification, but neither cine cameras nor projectors were necessarily electric.[7] The possibility of project-ing moving pictures depended finally on the development of photographic material flexible and strong enough to withstand transport through the various machines involved, the mechanisms of which were similar to those of other, older machines: the trans-port mechanism of the Lumières' *Cinématographe* was suggested by the shuttle of the sewing machine. Film is moved through cameras and projectors by mechanisms that convert the rotation of a motor or crank into the reciprocating movement of a pin or claw, so as to register duration as, and subsequently reconstruct it from, a series of still photographs. In a steam locomotive, the reciprocating movement of the pistons is converted into the rotation of the wheels, and hence into linear movement and the possibility of panoramic views from railway carriage windows. Photography and the passenger railway both date from the same period in the early nineteenth century: the Stockton and Darlington Railway in 1825, Joseph Niépce's photograph in 1826. One might see cinema as their belated combination.

The first of the various Lumière films known as *L'Arrivée d'un train en gare* was photographed in 1895 or early 1896. This film was not among those shown at the Lumières' first public screening in Paris, on 28 December 1895, at the Grand Café in the Boulevard des Capucines. The first mention of such a film, described as *L'Arrivée d'un train en gare d'un chemin de fer*, dates from 26 January 1896.[8] Several Lumière films of train arrivals are known to have been photographed with static cameras placed on station platforms, including Lumière catalogue no. 653, *L'Arrivée d'un train en gare de La Ciotat* (1897, or possibly late 1896), with which the earlier film is often confused. Whether or not *L'Arrivée d'un train en gare* really did disconcert audiences to the extent suggested by 'cinema's founding myth' – which seems unlikely[9] – the version in the British Film Institute's National Archive[10] is slightly unsettling. The camera is perhaps nearer to the edge of the platform than in similar films, and the approaching locomotive leans towards it, as if it might topple and crush the cinematographer.

In early cinema, movement of the camera relative to its tripod was unusual. There are a few films that comprise or include pans,[11] of which *The Great Ottawa Fire* (American Mutoscope and Biograph Company, 1900) and *Clifton Suspension Bridge* (British Mutoscope and Biograph Company, 1900) are examples. It must have been difficult to achieve a smooth movement, especially if the camera was cranked by hand, but cinematographers were quick to grasp the possibility of placing their otherwise static cameras on things that moved: boats, trains, trams and, later, motor cars. In this way, it was possible to extend the spectacle of a film a long way beyond what was visible in a static frame. The first moving-camera film is supposed to have been a view of Venice photographed from a moving gondola by Alexandre Promio (1868–1926) for the Lumière company in September or October 1896, and the first film made by placing a camera on a train was probably the Lumières' *Départ de Jérusalem en chemin de fer*, photographed by Promio in January or February 1897 – an oblique rearward view of a station platform from a departing train. Like many of Promio's films, it offers a glimpse of a space that would subsequently undergo considerable transformation. Palestine was then part of the Ottoman Empire. People on the platform watch the train depart, perhaps attracted by the camera. As the platform slips away, some of them raise their hats and wave.

Promio's travels for the Lumière company included two visits to the UK – in 1896, to London, and again in 1897 to London, Liverpool and Ireland. There are eight films of Liverpool, four of these – *Panoramas pris du chemin de fer électrique I–IV*[12] – a series of spectacular views of the docks photographed from the Liverpool Overhead Railway – the first elevated electric metropolitan railway in the world, which had opened in February 1893 and ran along the landward side of the docks until 1957. The films are especially striking in that they show to what extent large ocean-going sailing ships were still in everyday commercial operation. In this, they demonstrate what might be described as the temporal heterogeneity of the spaces glimpsed. The films are striking perhaps because they make this heterogeneity, unusually, very visible, and in doing so subvert the tendency of images, and films perhaps in particular, to offer illusory homogeneity, especially when depicting the spaces of the past. The railway's moving, cinematic view of the docks appears very modern, and the docks themselves were undergoing continual, mechanised development, but the ships convey the spatial experiences of an earlier, different time.

Seven of the twenty-five extant films[13] photographed by Promio in Ireland are of cavalry exercises. Of the remaining eighteen, eleven are railway panoramas photographed in urban, suburban and rural landscapes along the lines between Belfast and Dublin and from Dublin to Kingstown (now Dún Laoghaire), from which the mail-boats departed for Holyhead. The films are *Panorama de l'arrivée à Belfast*, *Panorama du départ de Belfast*, *Départ de Dammurey* (Dunmurry), *Lisburn*, *Départ de Surgan* (Lurgan), *Ligne de Belfast à Kingston I, II & III*, *Départ de la gare, panorama* (Dublin), *Soundy Mounts* (Sandymount) and *Arrivée à Kingston*. If the landscapes glimpsed in these films appear more familiar than the static-camera street scenes Promio photographed in Belfast and Dublin (as I would suggest they do), this is perhaps a consequence of both the moving-camera viewpoint and the modernity of some of their locations, the suburbs in particular. Some of the landscapes Promio photographed in Ireland are not far from those of Joyce's *Ulysses*,[14] which is set in 1904.

These Lumière films are *panoramas* – views resembling those of passengers from railway carriage windows (or panoramas that simulated them). In the evolution of the moving-camera film, the railway panorama was superseded by the *phantom ride*. Unlike *panorama*, the term *phantom ride* does not seem to have existed prior to its use to describe a certain kind of film, though it has since diffused into the language of horror fiction.[15] One might understand *phantom* merely as a modifier, meaning illusory, in which case railway panoramas can be and sometimes are described as phantom rides, but the term is more specific to a view in a direction close to that of the line of travel. In its strictest sense, a phantom ride is a film that looks forward from the front of a moving railway engine – a view then seldom encountered in ordinary experience, even by an engine driver. The combination of the camera's 'subjective' view and its conventionally inaccessible position suggests disembodied consciousness, though no one seems to know if this was a factor in the naming of the phantom ride, or when the term was first used, and by whom. In any case, in other variations of the moving-camera film the view is similarly oneiric, so that films in which the camera is looking backwards, or is located in a wagon halfway along the train, as well as films photographed from trams and cars in which the forward-facing view was unexceptional, have also been described as phantom rides, though perhaps not at the time they were first exhibited.[16]

On this basis, the earliest phantom ride was Promio's *Départ de Jérusalem en chemin de fer*, but the American Mutoscope and Biograph Company's *Haverstraw Tunnel* (1897) seems to have been the first film photographed from the front of a locomotive, and the first of many such rides produced by the Biograph companies. One of Biograph's four founders was William Kennedy-Laurie Dickson (1860–1935), who had previously developed and designed much of Thomas Edison's moving picture technology, and who in his work for Biograph became one of the most accomplished cinematographers of early cinema. The companies' films were photographed and exhibited in a large format of 68mm, as distinct from the usual 35mm: the 'Biograph' was an electric camera that, together with its stand and batteries, weighed over 2,000 pounds and ran at forty

Courtesy of the British Film Institute

Conway Castle – Panoramic View of Conway on the L & NW Railway (1898)

frames per second. It seems unlikely that it could have been mounted on the locomotive itself, but was perhaps instead placed in a wagon in front. Many of Biograph's films of this period offer a spatial quality not found in those of other producers,[17] so that one wonders if this was a characteristic of Dickson's approach.

Dickson, born in Brittany to British parents, had emigrated to the United States in 1879, joining Edison in 1883. In May 1897, he returned to Europe as the technical manager and cinematographer of the newly formed British Mutoscope and Biograph Syndicate (later Company),[18] travelling in the UK and Europe, and in South Africa during the Boer War. The British Biograph Company's films include *Conway Castle – Panoramic View of Conway on the L & NW Railway* (1898) and *Irish Mail – L & NW Railway – Taking Up Water at Full Speed* (1898), the southbound Holyhead-to-Euston boat train photographed passing through Bushey station from the rear of a train on a parallel track, which is overtaken by the express towards the end of the film. These films would have required extensive, precise collaboration with the railway company: the London and North Western appear to have been more often involved in early films than other railway companies. Another Biograph film was photographed on the same route – *Menai Bridge – The Irish Day Mail from Euston Entering the Tubular Bridge Over the Menai Straits* (1898) – and Charles Goodwin Norton's *Railway Traffic on the LNWR* (c.1897) was photographed from the platform of what was then Sudbury and Wembley station (now Wembley Central).

All these films survive in the collection of the British Film Institute's National Archive. There are other Biograph railway rides in the BFI's archive, most of them American Biograph titles.[19] If these were exhibited in the UK, as seems likely, this is one example among many of the transatlantic, westward orientation of much early cinema, at least in the UK,[20] which suggests a relationship between film and the prospect of emigration reminiscent of the role claimed by Oetterman for the moving panorama in the settlement of California. In American Biograph phantom rides such as *In the Canadian Rockies, near Banff* (1899) and *Railway Trip through Mountain Scenery and Tunnels* (1900), the movement of the trains suggests an anticipation one might imagine as characteristic of nearing the Pacific coast. Perhaps Biograph's international spread and Dickson's transatlantic journey were factors in Biograph's interest in the railway between Holyhead and London. A clue as to why this was the subject of so much attention – another film, *Phantom Ride: Menai Straits* (anon., c.1904), begins at about the same place as Biograph's *Conway Castle* – is offered by a remark of Charles Urban, an American film producer active in the UK: in an intertitle in *The Old Mauretania* (Charles Urban Trading Company, c.1910)[21] he writes that, when crossing the Atlantic, 'we usually took advantage of the Kingston–Holyhead route to reach London more quickly, by boarding a tender off Queenstown' (the port of Cork, now Cobh); i.e. he took a train to Dublin, the mailboat to Holyhead and the Irish Mail to Euston, suggesting that the train may have derived its status at least in part from its being patronised by transatlantic commuters. A comparable evocation of elsewhere was offered by British Biograph's *Through Miller's Dale (near Buxton, Derbyshire) Midland Rail* (1899), also known as *Through the Chee Tor Tunnel in Derbyshire*, a

Courtesy of the British Film Institute

Through Miller's Dale (near Buxton, Derbyshire) Midland Rail (1899)

three-take view from the front of a Midland Railway train as it passes though and beyond Miller's Dale Junction, where the branch to Buxton left the main Midland route between Derby and Manchester. Both the location and the railway journey were celebrated for touristic qualities that derived in part from the supposed resemblance of this and other places in Derbyshire to painterly landscapes in Italy.

The majority of UK railway rides date from before 1900, after which the electric tram was more often employed as a moving-camera platform.[22] All the British Biograph railway titles in the BFI's archive were photographed before Dickson left for South Africa in 1899. The only British Biograph moving-camera film in the archive that dates from after his return is *Panorama of Ealing from a Moving Tram* (July 1901), which was probably photographed by Dickson. By about 1903 he had left Biograph, returning to his profession as an electrical engineer. There are later American Biograph railway rides, including *The Georgetown Loop* (1901), photographed by Billy Bitzer, who later became D. W. Griffith's cinematographer.

Other film companies made phantom rides, though few are as spectacular as the large-format films produced by the Biograph companies. In the UK, both Cecil Hepworth's Hepwix and the Warwick Trading Company (the European branch of Maguire and Baucus set up by Urban) produced a number of examples. In Hepworth's *Through Three Reigns* (1922), a retrospective compilation of his early films, he refers (like Urban, in an intertitle) to 'stereoscopic cinema', meaning a feature of moving-camera films in which differential parallax suggests the illusion of depth. The film so introduced is *Thames River Scene* (1899), a panoramic, sideways view from a launch travelling downstream among other craft on the river at Henley, but the 'stereoscopic effect' is also characteristic of phantom rides. The stereoscope was one of the entertainments that preceded cinema, a competing medium which offered a three-dimensionality that cinema conventionally lacked, so that there would have been a potentially commercial aspect to Hepworth's interest in and realisation of 'stereoscopic' cinema.

Railway actualities are among the forms most closely associated with the period of early cinema. Their production declined with the development of narrative cinema, but the phantom ride played a significant role in this development. One of Hepworth's railway rides is *View from an Engine Front – Train Leaving Tunnel* (1899), which survives both as a film in its own right and as two of the three shots that comprise G. A. Smith's *The Kiss in the Tunnel* (also 1899). This was not the first film to attempt continuity editing, but is among the earliest successful examples in that it creates a convincing continuity from two quite separate camera subjects seen from different viewpoints. Smith made a studio shot in which a couple are seen in side view in a railway carriage compartment (like that of the fairground ride in *Letter from an Unknown Woman*). The window is dark, as if the train is in a tunnel, and the couple (Smith and his wife Laura) take the opportunity to embrace and kiss. As far as anyone knows, the scene survives only in combination with Hepworth's film, but it was advertised for sale as a potential addition to any phantom ride in which a train passed through a tunnel. Hepworth's film begins with a view from a stationary locomotive facing a tunnel entrance. A train emerges from the tunnel and passes the locomotive with the camera, which advances into the tunnel until the screen is entirely dark. At this point, Smith cut in his railway compartment scene, which is followed by the remainder of Hepworth's film – a moment of darkness in which a point of light appears and widens until the train emerges into daylight. The film's publicity took care to assert the propriety of the scene depicted, though viewers must surely have been aware of the dangers, real and imagined, that accompanied travel in isolated railway compartments.[23] There is another three-shot *Kiss in the Tunnel* made by the Riley Brothers and Bamforth companies in 1899 or 1900, in which the first and third shots are views of the train from beside the track. If this is a less successful example of film construction, it is perhaps because the forward movement in the first shot in the Hepworth/Smith film suggests that the carriage interior of the second shot is really in motion. Smith's insert functions as what became known as a cutaway, whereas the Riley/Bamforth film appears as three shots rather awkwardly joined together.

Despite the apparent decline in phantom ride production during the 1900s (in the UK at least) their exhibition continued. In 1904 George C. Hale, a former chief fire officer of Kansas City, began to exhibit phantom rides and other panoramas in spaces fitted out as replicas of American railway carriages, known initially as 'Hale's Tours and Scenes of the World'. At the height of their popularity, Hale's Tours had sites throughout the United States and in many other countries, opening in the UK in 1906 as 'Hale's Tours of the World'. In the tradition of the fairground ride, which continues today in simulations of space travel and other kinds of flight, Hale's Tours offered trips to 'the colonies or any part of the world (without luggage!)' for sixpence. Descriptions of their premises, in which the benches shook and the films were accompanied by the sounds of steam and whistles, recall the space described in Robert W. Paul's October 1895 patent application for a 'time machine'[24] that preceded his first screen projections. This was suggested by H. G. Wells's novel, and is another indication of the parallel between time travel and the railway panorama alluded to by Louis Jourdan's line in *Letter to an Unknown Woman*. In the UK, Hale's Tours had sites in London (one at 165 Oxford Street) and in other cities, and though the UK company does not appear to have survived for long,[25] at the height of their international popularity Hale's Tours were 'the largest chain of theatres exclusively showing films before 1906'.[26]

Tom Gunning has characterised cinema's early period as 'the cinema of attractions',[27] observing that after 1907 'the cinema of attractions does not disappear with the dominance of narrative, but rather goes underground, both into certain avant-garde practices and as a component of narrative films'.[28] In David Lean's *Brief Encounter* (1945), there is a curious echo of Promio's supposed first use of the moving camera. Celia Johnson ('Laura') is sitting by the window of a compartment on a train between 'Milford Junction' and 'Ketchworth', with a back-projected panorama of a near-dark English landscape outside and, in voice-over:

I stared out of that railway carriage window into the dark, and watched the dim trees and the telegraph posts slipping by, and through them I saw Alec and me – Alec and me – perhaps a little younger than we are now but just as much in love, and with nothing in the way [the panorama is now daylit] – I saw us in Paris [a superimposition appears], in a box at the opera, the orchestra was tuning up – then we were in Venice, drifting along the Grand Canal in a gondola with the sound of mandolins coming to us over the water – I saw us travelling far away together, all the places I've always longed to go – I saw us leaning on the rail of a ship looking at the sea and the stars – standing on a tropical beach in the moonlight with the palm trees sighing above us – then the palm trees changed into those pollarded willows by the canal before the level crossing – and all the silly dreams disappeared – and I got out at Ketchworth [the panorama has ended], and gave up my ticket and walked home as usual, quite soberly and without any wings, without any wings at all.

This sequence, with its added superimpositions and narration, confirms an interpretation of the railway panorama – suggested by Promio's first examples – as an image of the stream of consciousness. In 1913 Sigmund Freud wrote, famously, that psychoanalysts might usefully tell their patients to 'say whatever goes through your mind. Act as though, for instance, you were a traveller sitting next to the window of a railway carriage and describing to someone inside the carriage the changing views which you are seeing outside.'[29] The phantom ride, on the other hand, more particularly resembles Henri Bergson's 'predatory'[30] image of duration introduced in *Matter and Memory* (1896), in which the present is 'the invisible progress of the past gnawing into the future'.[31] The forward-moving cine camera, with its reciprocating claw and rotating shutter, might almost have been expressly devised to accomplish this 'gnawing'. Bergson's subsequent interpretation and critique of the cinematographic mechanism as a model of perception was to become a founding text for much contemporary film and other critical theory;[32] cinema's fragmentation of continuous duration is rarely so demonstratively enacted as by the railway and similar forward-moving films of the medium's first decade.

Gunning's distinction between 'the cinema of attractions' and what came later parallels other descriptions of the spatial transformations characteristic of the period. For Henri Lefebvre, 'around 1910 a certain space was shattered'[33] so that early cinema, arguably, offers a glimpse of this space just before (or possibly during) the period in which its 'shattering' occurred. One might even imagine the cinematographic mechanism itself as implicated in the 'shattering'.[34] As Walter Benjamin wrote, 'then came the film and burst this prison-world asunder by the dynamite of the tenth of a second'.[35] Benjamin's 'dynamite of the tenth of a second' is usually understood as a reference to montage; his essay mentions nothing of cinema earlier than the work of Gance and Vertov, but it seems to me at least as intriguing to imagine the prison-world burst asunder by juggernauts comprised of cine cameras, locomotives and electric trams, after whose passing nothing was ever the same again.

13

Imaging

On an overcast afternoon at the end of August 2008, I was cycling along Harrow Road, in north-west London, towards Harlesden. Passing Kensal Green Cemetery, I saw that a section of its high wall had collapsed, apparently not long before, so that passers-by could see in from the street for the first time, perhaps, since the wall was built in 1832, and the cemetery opened in January the following year. According to the newsletter of the Greater London Industrial Archaeology Society,[1] a hundred-metre section of the half-mile-long wall collapsed at around midnight on 30 August 2006. Most of the bricks fell into the cemetery, so that although many monuments were damaged, no one was injured. The wall varies between ten and twelve feet in height, and is a grade II listed structure, with stone copings and foundations five feet deep. It was built to keep out bodysnatchers.

I had not seen inside the cemetery since the early 1980s, when I visited a few times as an architectural tourist and would-be photographer. I was reminded of these visits, and that I had cycled along the same route once before on a Sunday afternoon in December 1980, when I set out to look for a place I had seen from a passing train a few days earlier. It was a north-facing hillside of allotments behind the corner of two streets of suburban houses, beyond the railway's bridge above the North Circular Road. I'm not sure why I went to look for the place on a bicycle, as it was quite a long way: I think it was probably because the vehicle I then owned was out of

Kensal Green Cemetery, 1980

action. The view had seemed to me a curiously northern-looking landscape to find in outer London, and I had thought it might be a subject for a photograph, which it was; but it led me to another, more compelling spatial subject for both a photograph and, a few months later, a first film, so that this earlier bicycle journey had been, for me, a significant, perhaps even life-changing, event.

It was not the first time that I had been to Harrow Road with a camera during that year. In May, I had resorted to going out very early to various parts of inner London in the hope of producing photographs of the urban landscape. One of these locations was Harrow Road, between the north end of Ladbroke Grove and Harlesden, the stretch that passes Kensal Green Cemetery. None of the resulting photographs, which included some of the cemetery, were very successful, although there is one, of the Harley Gospel Hall, at a bend of Harley Road, NW10, alongside the railway, of which the subject, at least, recalls some of O. G. S. Crawford's photographs of Southampton in the 1930s. It was not a very original photograph. In the view of the street in Google Earth, someone has posted what

Harley Road, London NW10, 1980

looks like a found colour transparency of the same subject,[2] seen from almost the same angle, at what looks like about the same date.

As far as I know, the literature of urban cycling is not very extensive. The bicycle is better established in a rural context. One of Alain Resnais's short films, *Châteaux de France* (1948), was made on a journey or series of journeys by bicycle. I am not much of a cyclist, but during the last decade I have been cycling as a means of getting around London. My bicycle dates from the early 1970s, or perhaps even earlier. I don't know exactly how old it is, but it is light and fast, and still has its original Weinmann centre-pull brakes, which were once considered glamorous. In my experience, if the journey is long enough and the road not too busy, the slightly detached condition of cycling can encourage lengthy associations of ideas or recollections. Walking, driving and looking out of the windows of trains, buses, aeroplanes, and so on, offer similar possibilities, but there seems to be something about the experience of riding a bicycle, the way in which one is both connected to and moving above the ground, that promotes a particular state of mind.

In August 2008, I was about two-thirds through a ten-month period of intermittent cinematography for another film, not yet complete as I write.[3] Apart from the collapsed state of the cemetery wall, and the memory of the previous journey, the ride did not lead to any very significant discovery, but it took place in a curious atmosphere of expectation, exacerbated by the weather, which recalled that described in the opening paragraphs of 'The Fall of the House of Usher', in which it was becoming clear that the 'worst' of the collapse of the financial sector was still to come, an apprehension confirmed by the failure of Lehman Brothers two weeks later, and subsequent events, all of which felt at the time as if they might constitute a historic *moment*. Any sense of justification that accompanied this long-predicted turn of events was tempered for me by fear of financial shipwreck, following a misunderstanding with my employer, and especially since I was riding to what advertisements describe as Europe's largest car supermarket, in Harlesden, where I had identified a possible replacement for my car. I had bought the car in 1995, when making a film called *Robinson in Space* (1997), which had involved journeys all over England, but did not believe I could realistically expect it to survive another annual test, due very shortly. It was an absurd destination for a bicycle ride, and an absurd time to be contemplating any major purchase, especially something as questionable as a car, but it would have been very difficult to continue the project without one. I had ridden across Kensington Gardens, up Ladbroke Grove, past the junction with Portobello Road, the setting for some of the final moments of *The Lavender Hill Mob* (1951) and parts of the film of Harold Pinter's *Betrayal* (1983), over the railway and the canal into Harrow Road which, with Harlesden, is a part of London I have come to associate with creative anxieties of one kind or another, some of them dating from the years immediately before and after 1979, when I was migrating unsteadily between careers, others earlier. A few days later, I decided to have the old car repaired, so that the journey, and much of the accompanying anxiety, were for nothing.

*   *   *

I arrived in London in September 1967 to become an architecture student, a few weeks after my seventeenth birthday. From around this time, I remember a view of the backs of houses, seen from a train as it passed through what I later identified as Willesden Junction station, and came to recognise as an indication of imminent arrival at Euston. Willesden Junction station is in Harlesden, not Willesden (as a former borough, Willesden, like Hornsey and West Ham, is difficult to place), and is very close to Harrow Road, which continues, crossing the North Circular Road, to Wembley and beyond. I am not sure when I first travelled by the route to Euston, but the journey would probably have been from Coventry, and was either just before or not long after starting university. I remember thinking what an endless undertaking it would be to rebuild the vast area of London's worn-out Victorian suburbs. I had travelled to London many times before, but usually either by car, when one mostly passes the fronts of houses, or by train to Paddington, and for some reason the house-backs of Ealing and Notting Hill had failed to prompt this sub-Orwellian response to urban dilapidation.

About eighteen months later, by then an unsettled and not very successful second-year student, not long after the occupation of the University of London Union building in Malet Street by locked-out LSE students and others, into which I had wandered from what then seemed an unfashionably technocratic Bartlett School of Architecture, I first visited Willesden Junction. I was living in surprisingly alienated circumstances with a friend with first-hand experience of student radicalism in Germany, in a small flat not far from Finchley Road and Frognal station, from which we sometimes travelled to Kew Gardens by the North London Line. At Willesden Junction the line is elevated as it crosses the Bakerloo line and the main lines running out of Euston, so the platforms are high up, with long views over the surrounding landscape. The North London Line crosses other radial main lines at several points as it circumnavigates the city, one of which can be seen from Copenhagen Fields, to the north of St Pancras station, in Alexander Mackendrick's film *The Ladykillers* (1955); but at Willesden

Junction the crossing coincides with a station, so that one can get off and properly explore the view. Beyond it, the line passes through a landscape of railway lines and other marginal territory, its longest stretch between stops. Attracted by the station and its surroundings, we set out on a day, I think, in February. I was reminded of this visit on reading, recently, that George Soros worked at Willesden Junction as a porter when a student at LSE in the 1950s. It was a time when I was managing on very little sleep, which no doubt exacerbated a euphoric experience of the land-scape that might have produced photographs, worthwhile or not, had it occurred to me to take a camera. A few years later, this would have been the primary aim of such a trip, but I did not then have any idea of a future making images, so that this first excursion was perhaps closer than any since to a *dérive*, although there were only two of us, and my clearest memory of it now is that it ended in the Galway Bay Restaurant, a celebrated café of which, sadly, I can find no trace. I think it was in Station Road. The meals were served on oval pictorial plates.

A few months later, we moved to an unfurnished flat in Kentish Town, a miserable post-war construction in a one-house gap made in a terrace by a bomb, near Kentish Town West station, also on the North London Line. I had found the flat advertised on a shop-window notice board. The rent was £7.00 a week. Six years later, in 1975, by which time I was in full-time professional employment, we moved again, to a flat overlooking Parliament Hill, where I stayed until January 1981, so that I lived on the North London Line for a total of about twelve years. From the flat in Hampstead, we could see the trains, both passenger and freight. Among the latter there were and still are shipments of nuclear waste from the power stations at Bradwell, now being decommissioned, and Sizewell, which join the main west coast route at Willesden Junction, en route to Sellafield.

In the late 1960s, the North London Line ran from Richmond to Broad Street, in the City. The trains were never very busy except, perhaps, on Saturday afternoons and other occasions when Arsenal were playing at home. They had three carriages, the central one of which had the Victorian no-corridor layout, with nine separate ten-seat compartments in any of which a person might find him- or herself isolated with several possibly ill-disposed fellow-passengers. These carriages were eventually modified in about 1980, in an attempt to reduce vandalism. In the mid 1970s, a style of large-scale multicolour calligraphic graffiti appeared on walls and other surfaces along the line, in which the two leading tags were 'Colonel Cav' and 'Columbo'. Not much of a television viewer, I didn't find out who Columbo was until later. I wondered if Colonel Cav was a character in a comic. Cav was, I thought, short for Cavendish, but it seems more likely that it was an abbreviation of cavalry. The trains ran every twenty minutes.

During the 1970s, I sometimes travelled on the line as a commuter from Highbury and Islington to Hampstead Heath, returning from the North East London Polytechnic's school of architecture in Walthamstow, where I taught one afternoon a week. Until then, I had encountered it mainly in connection with pleasure, sometimes just the pleasure of riding on the trains. I think this arises partly from the possibility the route offers to circumnavigate the city, and hence, perhaps, to become more familiar with something that is conventionally unknowable, inadequately experienced in a journey towards or away from the centre. In an essay 'Benjamin's Paris, Freud's Rome: Whose London?' (1999)[4] in which he argues that London is 'an essentially unsatisfactory and even frustrating linguistic structure' – assigning it, in the end, to Mrs Wilberforce, the leading character of *The Ladykillers* – Adrian Rifkin discusses the similar character of the 253 bus route, which then ran between Aldgate and Euston station, via Hackney. These routes recall the ancient practice of circumambulation, which has been carried out in many cultures, over many centuries, for a variety of purposes; recently, for example, by Iain Sinclair for *London Orbital* (2002).

Despite a succession of post-privatisation operators, the North London Line still seems to be known by its old name, and has been recognised as the prototype for and already-existing fragment of what one day might be a London orbital railway. In the 1980s it was added to the underground map, since when it has no longer seemed so exclusively the preserve of people who live and work along it. When Broad Street station was demolished, the route was extended east from Dalston to North Woolwich (via West Ham, where it crossed the northern outfall sewer, along the top of which is a path that leads to Beckton), and with this modification, the extraordinary industrial architecture of Silvertown and Beckton, and the Woolwich Ferry, became more easily accessible by train from other parts of London (at the time of writing, the line beyond Stratford is closed, to reopen as part of the Docklands Light Railway).[5] Crossing the ferry, a tourist could return to the centre through south London.

In 1979, I embarked on a postgraduate project in Peter Kardia's Department of Environmental Media at the Royal College of Art, where I began to make films and identified a canon of relevant texts, including Walter Benjamin's essay *Surrealism* (1929), in which I read that 'the true creative overcoming of religious illumination . . . resides in a profane illumination, a materialistic, anthropological inspiration' and that

> No one before these visionaries and augurs perceived how destitution – not only social but architectonic, the poverty of interiors, enslaved and enslaving objects – can be suddenly transformed into revolutionary nihilism. Leaving aside Aragon's *Passage de l'Opéra*, Breton and Nadja are the lovers who convert everything we have experienced on mournful railway journeys (railways are beginning to age), on godforsaken Sunday afternoons in the proletarian quarters of the great cities, in the first glance through the rain-blurred window of a new apartment, into revolutionary experience, if not action. They bring the immense forces of 'atmosphere' concealed in these things to the point of explosion. What form do you suppose a life would take that was determined at a decisive moment precisely by the street song last on everyone's lips?[26]

The Surrealist frisson, as a phenomenon, is described in literature (most explicitly in Louis Aragon's *Le Paysan de Paris*), but is experienced primarily as a subjective transformation of appearances. It is easy to associate it with the impulse to take a photograph, with *photogénie*, which Christopher Phillips describes as 'the mysterious transformation that occurs when everyday objects are revealed, as if anew, in a photograph or on the motion picture screen'.[7] While Surrealism may not have lived up to Benjamin's appreciation of its revolutionary potential, especially after the Second World War – Henri Lefebvre, writing in 1945, was particularly scathing[8] – the Surrealist preoccupation with transfiguration, and hence with the sacred, endures for us in the now-commonplace presence of everyday objects in art, and in the subjective transformation, radical or otherwise, of everyday surroundings, the most familiar manifestations of which are the various practices of urban exploration that have become so widely established, especially in London, since the early 1990s.

My image-making developed over several years. In 1977, I began assembling a collection of colour slides documenting 'found' architecture, and discovered a precedent for this in the Surrealists' adoption of particular locations and structures in Paris. The buildings I found were certainly interesting, but the pictures were not always very successful. I had embarked on the project with the intention of

Wormwood Scrubs, 1980

extending it with moving image media, either video or film, but had been discouraged by their poor definition compared to that of photographs, and by the limits of the camera's frame. I spent several months trying to develop a technique of architectural photography and eventually, on a trip to France, made a series of photographs which became the basis of an installation combining monochrome slides and spoken narration, which was followed by another made with photographs of a high wall behind the prison on Wormwood Scrubs. These two works were fairly well received – they were later included in an exhibition at the Tate Gallery[9] – and I recovered the project's initiative, which led me, a few weeks later, to cycle along Harrow Road.

When I arrived at the place I had seen from the train, I found that it was overlooked by an extraordinary structure, a metal footbridge I had not noticed as the train passed beneath it. About 200 metres long, it carries pedestrians over both the main line and a branch that passes underneath it, at an angle, in a tunnel. The longer of the bridge's two spans is oriented so that Wembley Stadium is framed between its parapets. The bridge's architecture suggested a renewed attempt at moving pictures: its long, narrow

Allotments, Wembley, 1980

View from footbridge, Wembley, 1980

walkway resembled the linearity of a film; its parapets framed the view in a ratio similar to the 4×3 of the camera, and its elaborate articulation, with several flights of steps, half landings and changes of direction, offered a structure for a moving-camera choreography which might include occasional panoramas.

The resulting film had two parts, the second of which was photographed a few weeks after the initial visit to the bridge, by walking a hand-held camera across it during a continuous ten-minute take. By this time, I think I had already decided to write fictional narration to accompany the picture. I discovered another footbridge, a square of walkways above the nearby junction of Harrow Road and the North Circular, with a spiral ramp at each corner, and photographed another ten-minute moving-camera walk, which became the first half of the film. This bridge was demolished in about 1992, when an underpass was built at the junction. The film was called *Stonebridge Park* (1981). Its narrative, such as it is, recalls the context, in the first part, and the immediate aftermath, in the second, of a theft committed by the narrator.

*   *   *

This rudimentary film was neither made nor conceived in a *moment*, but it originated in the unusual, unexpected experience that produced the photograph from which it evolved. Becoming more experienced in making images, I came to rely less on anything resembling the experiential phenomena of Surrealism, and became increasingly uncertain about their political significance. Exceptional moments of natural light seemed to offer similar conceptual transformations, and produced better pictures; for many who work with photographic media, the weather is not merely analogous with a state of mind. I have sometimes wondered whether I might have addressed these questions better if more of Henri Lefebvre's writing had been translated into English sooner than it was. *La Production de l'espace* was first published in 1974, but did not appear in English until Blackwell published Donald Nicholson-Smith's translation in 1991. I first encountered the book in 1994, before which I knew of Lefebvre and his relationship with the Situationists only from a brief mention in *Leaving the Twentieth Century* (1974), Christopher Gray's anthology of Situationist writing, an essential text for any would-be-literate punk rocker in the 1970s, in which I had found Gray's translation of part of Raoul Vaneigem's *Traité de savoir-vivre à l'usage des jeunes générations* (1967), known in English as *The Revolution of Everyday Life*, from which I often quoted:

> although I can always see how beautiful anything could be if only I could change it, in practically every case there is nothing I can really do. Everything is changed into something else in my imagination, then the dead weight of things changes it back into what it was in the first place.[10]

Nicholson-Smith's 1983 translation is closer to the original:

> though not everything affects me with equal force, I am always faced with the same paradox: no sooner do I become aware of the alchemy worked by my imagination upon reality than I see that reality reclaimed and borne away by the uncontrollable river of things.[11]

Lefebvre's assertion that 'the space which contains the realised preconditions of another life is the same one as prohibits what those preconditions make possible'[12] is a thought not unlike that in Vaneigem's paragraph. I wondered if the prohibition that Lefebvre identifies is sometimes suspended within the spaces of a film, and, if so, whether this might explain some of the attraction, and the seemingly utopian quality, of so much film space, and why some people are willing to devote so much time and effort to making films.

In Volume 3 of his *Critique of Everyday Life* (1981, published in English in 2005), Lefebvre wrote of

> Intense instants – or, rather, moments – it is as if they are seeking to shatter the everydayness trapped in generalised exchange. On the one hand, they affix the chain of equivalents to lived experience and daily life. On the other, they detach and shatter it. In the 'micro', conflicts between these elements and the chains of equivalence are continually arising. Yet the 'macro', the pressure of the market and exchange, is forever limiting these conflicts and restoring order. At certain periods, people have looked to these moments to transform existence.[13]

Lefebvre often writes of 'moments'. 'What is Possible', the final chapter of Volume 1 of the *Critique*, written in 1945, includes:

> Mystics and metaphysicians used to acknowledge that everything in life revolved around exceptional moments. In their view, life found expression and was concentrated in them. These moments were festivals: festivals of the mind or the heart, public or intimate festivals. In order to attack and mortally wound mysticism, it was necessary to show that festivals had lost their meaning, the power they had in the days when all their magnificence came from life, and when life drew its magnificence from festivals.[14]

Later, in *The Production of Space*, he identifies another kind of *moment*, in which 'around 1910 a certain space was shattered'.[15] This observation first appeared in English translation in 1990, its paragraph quoted by David Harvey in *The Condition of Postmodernity*, also published by Blackwell, and Harvey quoted it again in his afterword for Blackwell's edition of *The Production of Space*. Harvey's interest in the passage arises, I assume, from its identification of the beginning of a period that ended with the 'profound shift in the "structure of feeling"' that signalled the onset of postmodernity in the early 1970s, with the break-up of the Bretton-Woods fixed-exchange-rate system and the subsequent slide to neoliberalism. In the autumn of 2008, it began to seem possible that this period might be giving way to another.

If such moments of historical transition (however questionable their identification) open possibilities for creativity, for the moments to which, in Lefebvre's words, people have looked to transform existence (1910 was, among other things, the year in which Apollinaire invented the art of going for a walk[16]) it seemed strange that Surrealist and Situationist techniques – *flânerie*, the *dérive* and psychogeography – should have become the subject of so much attention (if they were not quite actually 'revived') in London during the 1990s. At the time, I suggested that their purpose had been overlooked: the *dérive* and psychogeography were conceived, in a more politically ambitious period, as preliminaries to the production of new, revolutionary spaces; in the 1990s they seemed more likely to be preliminary to the production of literature and other works, and to gentrification, the discovery of previously overlooked value in dilapidated spaces and neighbourhoods.

In an essay on 'contemporary London Gothic',[17] Roger Luckhurst suggested that the Gothic genre that he and others identified as characteristic of London in the 1990s was a response to 'that curious mix of tyranny and farce that constitutes London governance', particularly the dominance of the City of London, with its medieval peculiarities and its untiring pursuit of an ever more unequal, damaged world. Among the writers Luckhurst identified with the contemporary London Gothic, several have invoked the techniques of Situationist urbanism, as if the power of the financial sector is such that subjective re-imagination offered the only possibility for change that had become unattainable in other ways.

In 2008, cycling along Harrow Road, I did not encounter any explosion of the 'intense forces of "atmosphere"' that are undoubtedly concealed there, but unexpected memories of earlier discoveries, at a time when it seemed possible that a dysfunctional economic orthodoxy was finally collapsing, suggested that such experiences still have some value.

Acknowledgements

I am very grateful to everyone who commissioned or asked me to write the essays in this book, including, in chronological order, Michael O'Pray, Joe Kerr, Sarah Wigglesworth, Jeremy Till, Ann Gallagher, Kester Rattenbury, Mohsen Mostafavi, Nick Barley, Giles Lane, François Penz, Jane Rendell, Matthew Beaumont, Michael Freeman and Greg Hart, and to everyone involved in the book's production, particularly Leo Hollis and Rowan Wilson at Verso, who suggested it. I would also like to express my gratitude to Middlesex University, the Royal College of Art, the Arts and Humanities Research Council and the British Film Institute, for institutional support; Yehuda Safran, the late Ray Durgnat, Richard Wentworth, Jon Thompson, Barry Curtis, Ian Christie, Laura Mulvey, Michael Leaman, Al Rees, Mark Rappolt and Kitty Hauser, all involved in various ways; the late Cedric Price who, having been an inspiration to me since 1968, was such a generous interviewee and essay subject; and my partner, fellow-artist and sometime collaborator Julie Norris, whose contribution to these and other works of mine is very considerable.

A longer version of 'The Poetic Experience of Townscape and Landscape' was published in *Undercut* 3/4 (March 1982), pp. 42–8, reprinted in Nina Danino and Michael Mazière, eds, *The Undercut Reader* (London: Wallflower Press, 2003), pp. 75–83.

'Atmosphere, Palimpsest and Other Interpretations of Landscape' was published in *Undercut* 7/8 (Spring 1983), pp. 125–9, reprinted in Nina Danino and Michael Mazière, eds, *The Undercut Reader* (London: Wallflower Press, 2003), pp. 204–8.

'Port Statistics' was published in Iain Borden, Joe Kerr and Jane Rendell, with Alicia Pivaro, eds, *The Unknown City* (Cambridge MA: MIT, 2001), pp. 442–58.

'The Dilapidated Dwelling' was published in Sarah Wigglesworth and Jeremy Till, eds, *The Everyday and Architecture, Architectural Design Profile No. 134, Architectural Design* 68: 7–8 (1998), pp. 22–7.

'Popular Science' was first published in an exhibition catalogue *Landscape*, edited with an introduction by Ann Gallagher (London: British Council, 2000), pp. 60–7, reprinted in Anthony Kiendl, ed., *Informal Architectures: Space and Contemporary Culture* (London: Black Dog, 2008), pp. 32–7, and *Criticat 9*, March 2012, pp. 114–23, and abridged in the *Independent*, 6 March 2000.

'Architectural Cinematography' was published in Kester Rattenbury, ed., *This Is Not Architecture* (London: Routledge, 2002), pp. 37–44.

'London in the Early 1990s' was published in *AA Files 49: London, Post-Colonial City* (London: Architectural Association, 2003), pp. 20–4, and Joe Kerr and Andrew Gibson, eds, *London from Punk to Blair* (London: Reaktion 2003), pp. 353–61.

'London – Rochester – London' was published in Hans Ulrich Obrist, ed., *Re:CP* (Basel: Birkhäuser, 2003), pp. 168–85.

The Robinson Institute is one of a series of Diffusion e-books, *Species of Spaces* (2002), available at diffusion.org.

'The City of the Future' was published in *City* 7: 3 (November 2003), pp. 376–86.

'Film as Spatial Critique' was published in Jane Rendell, Jonathan Hill, Murray Fraser and Mark Dorrian, eds, *Critical Architecture* (London: Routledge, 2007), pp. 115–23.

'Phantom Rides: The Railway and Early Film' was published in Matthew Beaumont and Michael Freeman, eds, *The Railway and Modernity: Time, Space and the Machine Ensemble* (Bern: Peter Lang, 2007), pp. 69–84.

'Imaging' was first published in Matthew Beaumont and Gregory Dart, eds, *Restless Cities* (London: Verso, 2010), pp. 139–54, and an extract reprinted in Brian Dillon, ed., *Ruins* (London: Whitechapel Gallery/MIT, 2011), pp. 145–50.

Notes

Introduction

1 Roger Cardinal, 'Soluble City: The Surrealist Perception of Paris', in Dalibor Vesely, ed., *Surrealism and Architecture, Architectural Design Profile 11, Architectural Design* 48: 2–3 (1978), pp. 143–9.

2 Walter Benjamin, 'Surrealism: The Last Snapshot of the European Intelligentsia', in *One-Way Street and Other Writings*, transl. Edmund Jephcott, Kingsley Shorter (London: New Left Books, 1979), pp. 225–39, at p. 229.

3 *9H* was initiated in 1980 by a group including Wilfried Wang, later director of the Deutsches Architekturmuseum in Frankfurt, and Ricky Burdett, later founding director of the Architecture Foundation, Professor of Urban Studies at the London School of Economics, director of LSE Cities, etc.

4 There was an exhibition, *Czech Functionalism 1918–1938*, at the Architectural Association in 1987 (11 November–18 December); see Vladimír Šlapeta, *Czech Functionalism 1918–1938* (London: Architectural Association, 1987).

5 Published as 'Czech Perspective', *Building Design*, 13 March 1987.

6 See Stephen Daniels, 'Paris Envy: Patrick Keiller's *London*', *History Workshop Journal* 40 (1995), pp. 220–2.

7 'Port Statistics', in Iain Borden, Joe Kerr and Jane Rendell, with Alicia Pivaro, eds, *The Unknown City* (Cambridge MA: MIT, 2001), pp. 442–58.

8 Patrick Keiller, *Robinson in Space* (London: Reaktion, 1999).

9 *The City of the Future*, FACT, Liverpool, 28 May–27 June 2004; as part of *Londres, Bombay*, Le Fresnoy: Studio national des arts contemporains,

Tourcoing, 12 October–24 December 2006; and *The City of the Future*, BFI Southbank Gallery, 23 November 2007–3 February 2008. For an account of *Londres, Bombay*, see *Vertigo* 3: 6 (Summer 2007), pp. 42–3.

10 See also Patrick Keiller, *The Possibility of Life's Survival on the Planet* (London: Tate Publishing, 2012).

1. The Poetic Experience of Townscape and Landscape

1 Louis Aragon, 'On *Décor*', *Le Film*, September 1918, reprinted in Paul Hammond, ed., *The Shadow and its Shadow: Surrealist Writings on Cinema* (London: British Film Institute, 1978), pp. 28–31.

2 Edgar Allan Poe, *Selected Writings of Edgar Allan Poe*, ed. with an introduction by David Galloway (Harmondsworth: Penguin, 1980), pp. 179–88, at pp. 188, 179.

3 Charles Baudelaire, *Paris Spleen*, transl. Louise Varèse (New York: New Directions, 1970), p. x.

4 Guillaume Apollinaire, 'The False Amphion, or The Stories and Adventures of Baron d'Ormesan', in *The Wandering Jew and Other Stories*, transl. Rémy Inglis Hall (London: Rupert Hart-Davis, 1967).

5 See Bernard Tschumi, 'Architecture and Its Double', in Dalibor Vesely, ed., *Surrealism and Architecture, Architectural Design Profile 11, Architectural Design* 48: 2–3 (1978), pp. 111–16.

6 *Ten Days That Shook the University: Of Student Poverty Considered in its economic, political, psychological, sexual and, particularly, intellectual aspects, and a modest proposal for its remedy* (London: BCM/Situationist International, n.d. [1967]), p. 18.

7 Louis Aragon, *Paris Peasant*, transl. with an introduction by Simon Watson Taylor (London: Picador, 1980), pp. 128, 130.

8 Ibid., pp. 131–2.

9 André Breton, quoted from a radio interview in Simon Watson Taylor's introduction to his translation of Louis Aragon's *Paris Peasant* (London: Picador, 1980), pp. 9-10.

10 Georges Bataille, *Eroticism*, transl. Mary Dalwood (London: Marion Boyars, 1987), p. 22.

11 See Tschumi, 'Architecture and Its Double'.

12 Reprinted in *One-Way Street*, pp. 209–14, 215–22.

13 Walter Benjamin, 'The Work of Art in the Age of Mechanical Reproduction',

in *Illuminations*, ed. Hannah Arendt, transl. Harry Zohn (London: Fontana, 1973), p. 228; see also 'A Small History of Photography' (1931), in *One-Way Street*, pp. 240–57.

14 Tschumi, 'Architecture and Its Double', p. 115.

15 *Documents*, 1929, 6, p. 329. Bataille was *secrétaire générale* of *Documents* (1929, 1–7; 1930, 1–8), which usually included a section entitled either 'Chronique' (1929, 1; 1930, 4), 'Dictionnaire critique' (1929, 2), 'Chronique: Dictionnaire critique' (1929, 3) or 'Chronique: Dictionnaire' (1929, 4–7; 1930, 1, 2, 6, 7), with entries written by Bataille, Michel Leiris, Robert Desnos and others, many reprinted in *Encyclopædia Acephalica*, transl. Iain White and others, ed. with an introduction by Alastair Brotchie (London: Atlas Press, 1995), pp. 29–84.

16 From 'Self-Realisation, Communication and Participation', in *Leaving the Twentieth Century: The Incomplete Work of the Situationist International*, ed. and transl. Christopher Gray (London: Free Fall Publications, 1974), pp. 131–51, at p. 138 – a translation of Chapter 23 of Raoul Vaneigem's *Traité de savoir-faire à l'usage des jeunes générations*, known in English as *The Revolution of Everyday Life*. For a later translation, see p. 184.

17 Poe, *Selected Writings*, pp. 138–57, at p. 138.

18 Ibid., p. 143.

19 Baudelaire, *Paris Spleen*, 'The Double Room', pp. 5–7, at p. 6.

20 Vaneigem, 'Self-Realisation, Communication and Participation', in *Leaving the Twentieth Century*, p. 138.

21 Lewis Piaget Shanks, *Baudelaire: Flesh and Spirit* (London: Noel Douglas, 1930), p. 216, describing *Paris Spleen*.

22 Georges Bataille, 'Architecture', 'Dictionnaire critique', *Documents* No. 2, May 1929, p. 117.

2. Atmosphere, Palimpsest and Other Interpretations of Landscape

1 Daniel Defoe, *A Tour Through the Whole Island of Great Britain*, abridged, ed. and with an introduction by Pat Rogers (Harmondsworth: Penguin, 1979), p. 395.

2 Defoe, *A Tour Through the Whole Island of Great Britain*, pp. 491–3.

3 Thomas De Quincey, *The Confessions of an English Opium-Eater*, the revised version of 1856 (London: Folio Society, 1963), p. 90.

4 Ibid., p. 73.

5 Edgar Allan Poe, *The Domain of Arnheim*, in *Selected Tales* (London: Penguin, 1994), pp. 382–98, at pp. 386–7.

3. Port Statistics

1 *Nations for Sale*, a study of Britain's overseas image, was written by Anneke Elwes in 1994, for the international advertising network DDB Needham. Patrick Wright reported ('Wrapped in tatters of the flag', *Guardian*, 31 December 1994) that she found Britain 'a dated concept' difficult 'to reconcile with reality'.

2 The statement is part of Lord Henry Wotton's monologue to Dorian on their first meeting; see Oscar Wilde, *The Picture of Dorian Gray*, in *Complete Works*, general ed. J. B. Foreman (London: Collins, 1984), p. 32.

3 From 'Self-Realisation, Communication and Participation', p. 138.

4 See Enid Starkie, *Arthur Rimbaud* (London: Faber & Faber, 1961), p. 359.

5 *Port Statistics* (HMSO, London) is compiled annually by the Department of Transport. Most of the figures in this essay are for 1994, from the edition published in August 1995.

6 The UK's total port traffic in 1994 was 538 million tonnes. The ten major world ports in 1994 were: Rotterdam, 294 million tonnes; Singapore, 224 million freight tons; Shanghai, 166 million tonnes; Hong Kong, 111 million tonnes; Nagoya, 120 million freight tons; Antwerp, 110 million tonnes; Yokohama, 103 million freight tons; Marseille, 91 million tonnes; Long Beach, 88 million tonnes; and Busan, 82 million tonnes. Among major ports in the EU in 1994 were: Rotterdam, Antwerp, Marseille; Hamburg, 68 million tonnes; Le Havre, 54 million tonnes; London, 52 million tonnes; Amsterdam, 48 million tonnes; Genoa, 43 million tonnes; Dunkirk, 37 million tonnes; Zeebrugge, 33 million tonnes; and Bremen, 31 million tonnes.

7 Tony Lane, conversation with the author, April 1996.

8 As reported in the *Independent*, 21 January 1996.

9 The Scott inquiry investigated UK arms sales to Iraq during the Iran–Iraq war and thereafter. Its public hearings, between May 1993 and June 1994, were a continuing source of revelations about the conduct of ministers and officials of the Thatcher government. Its report was published in February 1996.

10 Sarah Hogg and Jonathan Hill, *Too Close to Call: Power and Politics, John Major in No. 10* (London: Little Brown, 1995), p. 125.

11 Edmund Burke, *A Philosophical Enquiry into the Origin of Our Ideas of the Sublime and Beautiful*, ed. Adam Phillips (Oxford: OUP, 1990), p. 36.

12 See Arthur Oswald, 'Country Homes and Gardens Old and New: West Green House, Hartley Wintney, Hampshire, the Seat of Evelyn, Duchess of Wellington', *Country Life*, 21 November 1936, pp. 540–5.

13 See for example the *Independent*, 12 May 1996.

4. *The Dilapidated Dwelling*

1 Office for National Statistics, reported in the *Guardian*, 7 October 1997. The figure was for unpaid work valued at the same rate as average paid employment.

2 ONS, reported in the *Guardian*, 7 October 1997.

3 Michael Ball, *Housing and Construction: A Troubled Relationship?* (Bristol: Policy Press, 1996), p. 1.

4 Philip Leather and Tanya Morrison, *The State of UK Housing* (Bristol: Policy Press, 1997), p. 21.

5 Central Statistical Office, *Regional Trends*, 1995 edition (London: HMSO), p. 94.

6 Ball, *Housing and Construction*, p. 7.

7 Ibid., p. 47.

8 Ibid., p. 8.

9 Florian Rötzer, 'Space and Virtuality: Some Observations on Architecture', in Bernd Meurer, ed., *The Future of Space* (Frankfurt: Campus Verlag, 1994), pp. 205–19, at pp. 205–6, 216–17.

10 Martin Heidegger, 'Building Dwelling Thinking', in *Poetry, Language, Thought*, transl. Albert Hofstadter (New York: Harper & Row, 1975), pp. 145–61, at p. 145.

11 Saskia Sassen, 'Economy and Culture in the Global City', in Meurer, *Future of Space*, pp. 71–89, at p. 74.

12 Kenneth Frampton, *Modern Architecture: A Critical History* (London: Thames & Hudson, 1980), p. 312.

13 Michel de Certeau, *The Practice of Everyday Life*, transl. Steven Randall (Berkeley: University of California Press, 1984), p. xvii.

14 Heidegger, 'Building Dwelling Thinking', p. 160.
15 Frampton, *Modern Architecture*, p. 311.
16 de Certeau, *Practice of Everyday Life*, pp. xi–xii, xx, xxiii–iv.
17 André Breton, quoted from a radio interview in Simon Watson Taylor's introduction to his translation of Louis Aragon's *Paris Peasant* (London: Picador, 1980), p. 10.

5. Popular Science

1 Robert Burton, *The Anatomy of Melancholy*, ed. Holbrook Jackson, introductions by Holbrook Jackson and William H. Gass (New York: New York Review Books, 2001), p. 47.
2 Henri Bergson, *Laughter: An Essay on the Meaning of the Comic*, transl. Cloudesley Brereton, Fred Rothwell (London: Macmillan, 1911), reprinted in *Comedy*, ed. with an introduction by Wylie Sypher (Baltimore: Johns Hopkins University Press, 1980), pp. 59–190, at pp. 157–8.
3 Roman Jakobson, *Language in Literature*, ed. Krystyna Pomorska and Stephen Rudy (Cambridge MA: Harvard University Press, 1987), pp. 368–78, at pp. 368–9.
4 Michal Bregant, 'Poems in Light and Darkness: The Films and Non-Films of the Czech Avant-Garde', *Umění* XLIII: 1–2 (1995), pp. 52–5.
5 de Certeau, *Practice of Everyday Life*, pp. xi, xxiii–xxiv. The quotation is from Witold Gombrowicz, *Cosmos*, transl. Eric Mosbacher (London: MacGibbon & Kee, 1967), p. 126.

6. Architectural Cinematography

1 *The Production of Space*, transl. and ed. Donald Nicholson Smith (Oxford: Blackwell, 1991), pp. 189–90.
2 Reprinted in Paul Hammond, ed., *The Shadow and its Shadow: Surrealist Writings on Cinema* (London: British Film Institute, 1978), pp. 28–31.
3 Louis Aragon, *Paris Peasant*, transl. with an introduction by Simon Watson Taylor (Boston: Exact Change, 1994), pp. 113–15.
4 Reprinted in *Kuleshov on Film: Writings of Lev Kuleshov*, transl. and ed. Ronald Levaco (Berkeley: University of California Press, 1974), pp. 51–2.
5 See, for instance, Eric de Maré, *Photography* (London: Penguin, 1968) and *Architectural Photography* (London: Batsford, 1975); Margaret S. Livingstone,

'Art, Illusion and the Visual System', *Scientific American* 258: 1 (January 1988), pp. 78–85.

6   *The End* (1986), *Valtos* (1987) and *The Clouds* (1989), the first two independently produced with support from the Arts Council of Great Britain, the third for the British Film Institute.

7   See, for instance, de Maré, *Architectural Photography*.

8   The 35mm film frame was initially standardised with an aspect ratio of 1.33:1 (the ratio of many of Turner's best-known works, often 48″ × 36″) and then, for sound, in 'Academy' ratio – 1.37:1. With the advent of television, also 1.33:1, wider ratios were introduced in cinema. These were initially achieved using anamorphic lenses which 'stretched' the 4×3 frame laterally. More recently, however, widescreen films have been made increasingly with conventional lenses, the frame masked to achieve the wider ratios, typically 1.66:1 or 1.85:1. A large proportion of the frame is not used, and the image has to be magnified more in projection. To avoid this, and to enable the cinema, television and video versions of the film to be the same, the older Academy ratio was used. Also, as all the prints were made from the original camera negative, the picture was unusually sharp.

9   The film documents IRA bomb damage, the general election, the problems of the royal family, the ERM crisis and the parliamentary debates about the Maastricht Treaty, and two big demonstrations that followed the government's announcement of pit closures.

10 Larry Sider, also known for his work with Laura Mulvey and Peter Wollen, and the Brothers Quay.

11 *Robinson in Space* (1997) and *The Dilapidated Dwelling* (2000).

7. London in the Early 1990s

1   Alexander Herzen, *Ends and Beginnings*, transl. Constance Garnett (Oxford: OUP, 1985), p. 431.

2   See Cecily Mackworth, *English Interludes: Mallarmé, Verlaine, Paul Valéry, Valéry Larbaud in England, 1860–1912* (London: Routledge & Kegan Paul, 1974).

3   The story of Apollinaire's affair and his visits to London is told in John Adlard, *One Evening of Light Mist in London* (Edinburgh: Tragara Press, 1980), and alluded to in Apollinaire's *L'Emigrant de Landor Road* and other poems in

Alcools. The Playdens lived at 75 Landor Road. In 1992, an unofficial blue plaque commemorated this. Landor Road is named after the poet Walter Savage Landor, and *Landor's Cottage* is a story by Edgar Allan Poe.

4 Enid Starkie, *Arthur Rimbaud* (London: Faber & Faber, 1961).

5 Charles Baudelaire, *Journaux intimes: mon coeur mis à nu*, XXI (36): 'Étude de la grande maladie de l'horreur du domicile.'

6 Including, for example, the passage in *Paris Spleen*, transl. Louise Varèse (New York: New Directions, 1970), 'Any Where Out Of The World', pp. 99–100, at p. 99: 'Life is a hospital where every patient is obsessed by the desire of changing beds. One would like to suffer opposite the stove, another is sure he would get well beside the window. It always seems to me that I should be happy anywhere but where I am, and this question of moving is one that I am eternally discussing with my soul.'

7 This might be confirmed by this sequence's being the only part of the film with anything like direct sound. The picture was shot mute and all the sound was post-synchronised, but while I was editing the carnival footage, the film-maker Patricia Diaz, who was working in the same building, happened to walk past the open door of the cutting room and recognise the subject. She had been on the float with a video camera, and we subsequently arranged to use some of her sound. The film later developed a following among Colombians in London.

8 Richard Bate, Richard Best and Alan Holmans, eds, *On the Move: Housing Consequences of Migration* (York: Joseph Rowntree Foundation, 2000), p. 6.

9 Paul Dave, 'The Bourgeois Paradigm and Heritage Cinema', *New Left Review* I/224 (July–August 1997), pp. 111–26.

10 Ellen Meiksins Wood, *The Pristine Culture of Capitalism: A Historical Essay on Old Regimes and Modern States* (London: Verso, 1991), p. 18, pp. 108–9.

8. London – Rochester – London

1 No problem here – plenty of copies.

2 The colour was jade green.

3 The fiftieth anniversary of the Festival of Britain was in 2001.

4 See 'Flatscape with Containers', Reyner Banham, *New Society*, 17 August 1967, in which Banham admired Price's application of 'container technology, near enough' in the Potteries Thinkbelt.

5   Nearby is Ebbsfleet, the site for a future Channel Tunnel Rail Link station, and the centre of one of the biggest concentrations of house-building in Europe.

6   Joseph Conrad, *Heart of Darkness* (London: Penguin, 1985), p. 30. Conrad's narrator tells his story on a boat moored off Gravesend, beginning: "'And this also,' said Marlow suddenly, "has been one of the dark places of the earth.'"

7   Charles Dickens, *The Posthumous Papers of the Pickwick Club* (London: Penguin, 1999), p. 29.

8   Sergei Eisenstein, 'Dickens, Griffith and the Film Today' (1944), in *Film Form: Essays in Film Theory*, ed. and transl. Jay Leyda (New York: Harcourt, Brace, 1949).

9   A Pickwick motif, first mentioned in Chapter 2.

10 Dickens, *The Posthumous Papers of the Pickwick Club*, p. 30.

11 For more on Staffordshire, see Borges's *The Garden of Forking Paths*.

12 As W. G. Sebald noted, of Dunwich: 'A strikingly large number of our settlements are oriented to the west and, where circumstances permit, relocate in a westward direction. The east stands for lost causes.' *The Rings of Saturn* (London: Harvill, 1998), p. 159.

9. The Robinson Institute

1   During the same period, a large number of bars were bought by banks – in March 2001, the Japanese investment bank Nomura owned 5,585 pubs in the UK, and it was announced that Morgan Grenfell (a subsidiary of Deutsche Bank) had bought Whitbread's estate of 2,998.

2   T. H. Mawson, *The Life and Work of an English Landscape Architect* (London: Richards, 1927), p. 344.

3   *Robinson in Space* (1997).

4   This was a Whitbread *Travel Inn* at Orrell, near Wigan, a couple of hundred yards from junction 26 of the M6 motorway.

5   *The Dilapidated Dwelling* (2000).

10. The City of the Future

1   However, in *Building Futures*, an analysis of the future of the construction industry produced by the UK's Royal Institute of British Architects (RIBA) and the Commission for Architecture and the Built Environment

(CABE) in July 2003, academics and professionals imagined five scenarios, in one of which Will Hughes of Reading University predicted that, by 2023, 'technological advances will create an industry in which procurement of new buildings is fully automated and no role is left for architects', and that old buildings will be 'quickly replaced by shiny new standardised products that can be maintained by a semi-skilled work-force'. Similar transformations were anticipated during the 1990s, but seem no nearer today.

2 See, for instance, Philip Leather and Tanya Morrison, *The State of UK Housing* (Bristol: Joseph Rowntree Foundation, 1997).

3 Including business, retail and leisure parks, hypermarkets, shopping malls, distribution estates, container ports, prisons, hotels, airports, etc. Rem Koolhaas characterises these as 'Junkspace', 'the sum total of our current achievement; we have built more than did all previous generations put together'. Koolhaas probably spends a lot of time in airports: in much of the UK and 'old Europe', Junkspace appears to be largely peripheral to older spaces.

4 Jane Jacobs, *The Death and Life of Great American Cities* (London: Penguin, 1964), p. 201.

5 The photographs of Bernd and Hilla Becher, for example.

6 de Certeau, *Practice of Everyday Life*, pp. xxiii–xxiv.

7 Adolf Loos, in his essay *Architecture* (1910) wrote: 'The house has to please everyone, contrary to the work of art, which does not. The work of art is a private matter for the artist. The house is not. The work of art is brought into the world without there being a need for it. The house satisfies a require-ment. The work of art is responsible to none; the house is responsible to everyone. The work of art wants to draw people out of their state of comfort. The house has to serve comfort. The work of art is revolutionary; the house is conservative. The work of art shows people new directions and thinks of the future. The house thinks of the present.' Transl. Wilfried Wang with Rosamund Diamond and Robert Godsill, in Wilfried Wang, Yehuda Safran with Mildred Budny, eds, *The Architecture of Adolf Loos* (London: Arts Council of Great Britain, 1985), pp. 107–8.

8 This is not so much a reference to Heidegger's 'Poetically Man Dwells', etc., as to the dilemmas presented to child-rearing households of moderate means by some contemporary cities, especially London.

9   At least in the West, the global consumer economy's locations for production, distribution and consumption are typically suburban or 'rural', while global finance is increasingly centralised in the City of London and similar 'world cities'.

10 See, for instance, Dudley Baines, *Migration in a Mature Economy* (Cambridge: CUP, 1985), pp. 1, 3.

11 London's City and South London Railway, which became part of the Northern Line.

12 The first network was in Richmond, Virginia, in 1888. In the UK, electric trams date mostly from the early 1900s.

13 Such as, for instance, the Lumière company's *Panoramas pris du chemin de fer électrique*, photographed from the Liverpool Dock Railway by Alexandre Promio in 1897.

14 For example, when the original Tate Gallery at Millbank opened in 1897, it had cost its patron, Sir Henry Tate, £105,000 to build. In a comparison based on retail prices, this is 'equivalent' to about £6 million today; in a comparison based on average wages and salaries, to about £20 million. Tate's original gallery was only the first phase of the present gallery, about a fifth of its current area, but the recent refurbishment alone cost £30 million. In the early 1900s, a new three-bedroom house in a London suburb could be bought for about £300 – 'equivalent' to about £18,000 (prices) or £60,000 (wages) – of which about £50 would have been the cost of the site. In 1914, only 10 per cent of homes were owner-occupied.

15 A UK government-appointed task force headed by Sir John Egan, BAA chief executive, produced its report *Rethinking Construction* in July 1998, describing an industry that 'produces poor profits, fails to invest, and treats its employees as a commodity to be hired and fired and given dirty, unsafe conditions to work in'. Construction was rated so poorly by the City that the stock market capitalisation of the entire quoted sector was only £12 billion – only 75 per cent of the (then) value of retailer Marks and Spencer.

16 A week's wage for a bricklayer was just over £2 (40s7d) in 1914, £3.67 (73s5d) in 1924 – *British Labour Statistics, Historical Abstract 1886–1968*.

17 Reprinted in Paul Hammond, ed., *The Shadow and its Shadow: Surrealist Writings on Cinema* (London: British Film Institute, 1978), p. 29.

18 Lefebvre identifies a 'conceptual triad' of spatial practice, representations of space, and representational spaces ('the perceived–conceived–lived triad'). Spatial practice is 'a close association, within perceived space, between daily

reality (daily routine) and urban reality (the routes and networks which link up the places set aside for work, "private" life and leisure)'. Representations of space are 'conceptualised space, the space of scientists, planners, urbanists, technocratic subdividers and social engineers, as of a certain type of artist with a scientific bent – all of whom identify what is lived and what is perceived with what is conceived'. Representational spaces are 'space as directly *lived* through its associated images and symbols, and hence the space of "inhabitants" and "users", but also of some artists and perhaps of those, such as a few writers and philosophers, who *describe* and aspire to do no more than describe. This is the dominated – and hence passively experienced – space which the imagination seeks to change and appropriate.' *The Production of Space*, transl. Donald Nicholson-Smith (Oxford: Blackwell, 1991), pp. 38–9. Lefebvre's book was first published in 1974, and was quoted in David Harvey's *The Condition of Postmodernity*, which appeared in 1990, and in which 'representational spaces' is translated as 'spaces of representation', and the three concepts are stated slightly differently (pp. 218–19).

19 Lefebvre, *Production of Space*, pp. 189–90.

20 Cinema, for example, conventionally represents city space with relatively low levels of traffic noise, if only so that the dialogue can be heard. The transformative effect of such changes in the actual aural environment can sometimes be noticed during road closures, political demonstrations, or other unusual circumstances.

21 Kenneth Frampton, *Modern Architecture: A Critical History* (London: Thames & Hudson, 1980); both passages are quoted on p. 278.

22 T. Jackson, N. Marks, J. Ralls and S. Stymne, *Sustainable Economic Welfare in the UK, 1950–1996* (London: NEF, 1997), p. 28.

23 Or, as Stan Douglas writes: 'That the stage for the global dominance of financial markets was abruptly set by the 1973 oil crisis – and fully dressed with the collapse of the Bretton Woods system shortly thereafter – is proof that, far from being a dead zone between the emancipatory utopias of the 1960s and the protectionist greed of the 1980s, the current distribution of power is the secret meaning of the 1970s.' *Journey into Fear* (London: Serpentine Gallery, 2002), p. 136.

24 See, for instance, David Harvey, *The Condition of Postmodernity* (Oxford: Blackwell, 1990), pp. 39, 54.

25 *If. . . .* was photographed by Miroslav Ondříček.

11. Film as a Special Critique

1 For more on the implications of electronic media for experience of moving images, see Laura Mulvey, *Death 24x a Second: Stillness and the Moving Image* (London: Reaktion, 2005).

2 By 'film', I mean film footage in which architecture and landscape are visible, rather than particular films about architecture and landscape. After about 1920, such footage is perhaps more widely encountered in feature narratives, especially after 1945, when location cinematography began to become more common.

3 *The City of the Future*, a research project (2002–05) based at the Royal College of Art, London. See vads.ac.uk.

4 Tom Gunning, 'The Cinema of Attractions: Early Film, Its Spectator and the Avant-Garde', in Thomas Elsaesser, ed. (with Adam Barker), *Early Cinema: Space, Frame, Narrative* (London: BFI, 1990), pp. 56–62.

5 Gunning, 'The Cinema of Attractions', p. 57.

6 See Tony Rayns, 'Death at Work: Evolution and Entropy in Factory Films', in Michael O'Pray, ed., *Andy Warhol Film Factory* (London: BFI, 1989), p. 164.

7 Lefebvre, *The Production of Space*, p. 25.

8 David Harvey, *The Condition of Postmodernity* (Oxford: Blackwell, 1990), p. 266.

9 Stephen Kern, *The Culture of Time and Space 1880–1918* (Cambridge, MA: Harvard University Press, 1983), p. 5.

10 John Berger, 'The Moment of Cubism', *The Moment of Cubism and Other Essays* (London: Weidenfeld & Nicholson, 1969), p. 6.

11 Ibid., p. 5.

12 According to Kern, 30 million emigrants left Europe between 1890 and 1914. *The Culture of Time and Space*, p. 220.

13 Reyner Banham, *Theory and Design in the First Machine Age* (London: Architectural Press, 1960), p. 14.

14 Ibid., p. 67.

15 Ibid., p. 317.

16 Ibid., p. 311.

17 Ibid., p. 66.

18 Benjamin, 'The Work of Art in the Age of Mechanical Reproduction', p. 238.

19 Ibid., p. 228.

20 Average income in employment increased about three times as much as indices of retail prices. The cost of housing has generally increased more than average income.

21 See, for instance, Jackson et al., *Sustainable Economic Welfare in the UK, 1950-1996*, who report that the UK's Index of Sustainable Economic Welfare (ISEW) peaked in 1976, and has since dropped by 25 per cent to the level of the 1950s, increases in GDP per head etc. having been offset by environmental decline, increased inequality and other factors. Similar patterns have been found in other advanced economies, notably the United States.

22 See Kern, *Culture of Time and Space*, p. 157.

23 Harvey, *Condition of Postmodernity*, p. 276; see also Camillo Sitte, *City Planning According to Artistic Principles* (London: Phaidon, 1965), first published in Vienna in 1889.

24 Harvey, *Condition of Postmodernity*, p. 276.

25 Ibid., p. 277.

26 See, for instance, Georg Simmel, 'The Metropolis and Mental Life', in *On Individuality and Social Forms* (Chicago: University of Chicago Press, 1971), pp. 324–9. The essay was first published in 1903.

27 Among over fifty urban actuality films from the years 1895–1903, I have encountered only one in which cars appear: *Busy London – Traffic Passing in Front of the Bank of England and Mansion House* (Walturdaw, 1903), in which there are two cars, among a multitude of horse-drawn vehicles and pedestrians. In contrast, the surviving incomplete print of Cecil Hepworth's *City of Westminster* (1909) begins with a ninety-second moving-camera view photographed by Gaston Quiribet from a car that drives from the north end of Whitehall, up the east side of Trafalgar Square into St Martin's Lane. The traffic includes cars, horse buses, horse-drawn carts and vans, bicycles, hackney cabs, motor taxis, a steam lorry, and many people crossing the road between them. After the mid 1900s, such shots are rare.

12. The Phantom Rides

1 Stephan Oetterman, *The Panorama: History of a Mass Medium* (New York: Zone, 1997), pp. 314, 323, 325.

2 Ibid., pp. 66, 323, 340.

3 Charles Dickens, 'The American Panorama', *Examiner*, 16 December 1848, quoted in Oetterman, *Panorama*, p. 329. See also Bernard Comment, *The Panorama* (London: Reaktion, 1999), p. 63. Comment suggests that Banvard's original panorama could not have measured much more than 400 metres (though further scenes were added later).

4 Wolfgang Schivelbusch, *The Railway Journey: The Industrialisation of Time and Space in the Nineteenth Century* (Leamington Spa: Berg, 1986), p. 62.

5 Oetterman, *Panorama*, p. 179; Comment, *Panorama*, p. 74. The exhibit was funded by the Compagnie Internationale des Wagons-Lits.

6 Stefan Zweig, *Letter from an Unknown Woman*, transl. Eden and Cedar Paul (London: Cassell, 1933), first published in 1922 as *Brief einer Unbekannten*.

7 See, for example, Harvey, *Condition of Postmodernity*, and Stephen Kern, *The Culture of Time and Space 1880–1918* (Cambridge, MA: Harvard University Press, 1983). For more on early film see, for example, Stephen Herbert and Luke McKernan, eds, *Who's Who of Victorian Cinema: A Worldwide Survey* (London: British Film Institute, 1996) and the accompanying website at victorian-cinema.net; Richard Abel, ed., *Encyclopedia of Early Cinema* (London: Routledge, 2005); and Ian Christie, *The Last Machine: Early Cinema and the Birth of the Modern World* (London: BBC/BFI, 1994).

8 Martin Loiperdinger, 'Lumière's Arrival of the Train: Cinema's Founding Myth', *The Moving Image: The Journal of the Association of Moving Image Archivists* 4: 1 (Spring 2004), pp. 89–118, at p. 101.

9 Loiperdinger, 'Lumière's Arrival of the Train', pp. 89–101.

10 According to the BFI's database, this is Lumière catalogue no. 653. It also matches Loiperdinger's description of no. 653. Loiperdinger mentions two other Lumière train arrivals, no. 8 (at Villefranche-sur-Saône) and no. 127 (at Lyon), and that three versions of *L'Arrivée d'un train de La Ciotat* are known to have existed, of which no. 653 is the latest. The La Ciotat train arrival captioned as Lumière no. 653 on many internet sites is not the film described by the BFI and Loiperdinger (there are, for instance, no female Lumière family members on the platform).

11 The cinematographers' term 'pan' is an abbreviation of panorama, but a pan is usually the result of rotating the camera laterally whereas a 'panorama' is the result of sideways or other movement of the camera's support.

12 In the CNC's compilation in the BFI's National Archive, the films are edited together in non-topographical order. They are views from southbound trains

travelling from what was then the north end of the docks, passing Canada Dock (*III*), Sandon Dock (*IV*), Victoria, Waterloo and Prince's Docks (*II*) and George's, Canning, Salthouse and Albert Docks (*I*), so that the topographical order would be *III, IV, II, I*. By 1904, George's Dock had been filled in. Promio's other Liverpool films are *Church Street, Lime Street, Entrée dans Clarence Dock* and *La Rade*, a view across the river from a slow-moving viewpoint near the present pier head, with a ship moving slowly upstream.

13 The BFI's National Archive holds five compilation reels of Lumière films, presented to the BFI in 1995 by the Centre National de la Cinématographie (CNC) on the occasion of the centenary of cinema, which are intended to include all extant films made by the company in the UK. One of the two films known as *Pont de la tour* is not included (a view from a boat moving downstream beneath Tower Bridge), perhaps because it was already held by the BFI (the *Pont de la tour* in the CNC compilation is a view of pedestrian and horse-drawn traffic on the bridge seen from the carriageway's pavement).

14 One might be tempted to look for the landscape of 'Bloom Cottage', of the episode 'Ithaca', in Promio's panoramas.

15 Nigel Kneale's television series *Quatermass and the Pit* includes a reference to 'the wild hunt . . . the phantom ride of witches and devils'.

16 British Biograph's forward-facing tram ride through Ealing, for example, is called *Panorama of Ealing from a Moving Tram* (1901).

17 The Library of Congress's memory.loc.gov offers the opportunity to compare twenty-five Biograph and twenty Edison films of New York in 1898–1906. Biograph's films include some particularly successful depictions of spatial or architectural subjects (for example, *Beginning a Skyscraper*), while Edison's often seem more interested in performance.

18 See Barry Anthony and Richard Brown, *A Victorian Film Enterprise: The History of the British Mutoscope and Biograph Company, 1897–1915* (Trowbridge: Flicks Books, 1999).

19 American Biograph phantom rides in the BFI's archive include *Across Brooklyn Bridge* (1899), *The Crookedest Railroad Yard in the World* (1897), *From Vaudreuil to St Anne's* (1900), *In the Canadian Rockies, near Banff* (1899), *Into the Catskills: a Race for a Siding* (1906), *Railway Trip through Mountain Scenery and Tunnels* (1900), *A Ride on a Switchback* (1900, or c.1898), *Victoria Jubilee Bridge, St Lawrence River, Canada* (1900) and *The Georgetown Loop* (1901).

20 This seems to have been fairly widespread: in a Mitchell and Kenyon tram-ride film of Nottingham, the camera dwells on a wall of poster advertisements, the largest of which is for the North American Animated Photo Co., a UK company that commissioned many of Mitchell and Kenyon's films. Another of Mitchell and Kenyon's customers was A. D. Thomas, who traded as the Thomas-Edison Animated Photo Co. and sometimes billed himself as 'Edison-Thomas'.

21 Urban's intertitles refer to the sinking of the *Lusitania* in 1915, so must have been added later.

22 Many of the UK's tram networks were electrified during the late 1890s and early 1900s. Horse trams had not offered such a steady movement, but the top of a tram was perhaps more accessible than the front of a locomotive, and the streets a more active camera subject, offering the possibility that people photographed would become the film's paying customers.

23 For the distinction between the American and European pattern of railway carriage and the dangers of the latter, see Schivelbusch, *The Railway Journey*, Chapter 5, 'The Compartment' (pp. 70–88) and Chapter 6, 'The American Railroad' (pp. 89–112), particularly 'The New Type of Carriage' (pp. 98–103) and 'River Steamboat and Canal Packet as Models for the American Railroad Car' (pp. 103–7).

24 See John Barnes, *The Beginnings of the Cinema in England, Vol. 1: 1894–1896* (Exeter: University of Exeter Press, 1998), pp. 38–41.

25 Hales Tours of the World Ltd was superseded by Hales Tours of the World (UK) Ltd, for which a receiver was appointed in 1908 (see Ian Christie et al. *London Project*, at londonfilm.bbk.ac.uk).

26 Tom Gunning, 'The Cinema of Attractions: Early Film, Its Spectator and the Avant-Garde', in Elsaesser and Barker, *Early Cinema*, pp. 56–62, at p. 58.

27 Gunning, 'Cinema of Attractions', pp. 56–62.

28 Ibid., p. 57.

29 Sigmund Freud, 'On Beginning the Treatment (Further Recommendations on the Technique of Psycho-Analysis I)' (1913), *The Standard Edition of the Complete Psychological Works* (London: Vintage, 2001), Vol. 12, pp. 123–44, at p. 135.

30 See Kern, *Culture of Time and Space*, p. 43.

31 Henri Bergson, *Matter and Memory*, transl. N. M. Paul and W. S. Palmer (New York: Zone, 1991), p. 150.

32 See, for example, Bergson, *Matter and Memory*, p. 150: 'Your perception, however instantaneous, consists then in an incalculable multitude of remembered elements', which might resemble duration's fragmentation into individual frames of film, at odds with Bergson's preceding affirmation of continuity on p. 149: 'Either, then, you must suppose that this universe dies and is born again miraculously at each moment of duration, or you must attribute to it that continuity of existence which you deny to consciousness, and make of its past a reality which endures and is prolonged into its present.'

33 Lefebvre, *Production of Space*, p. 25.

34 Perhaps not so much in terms of Bergson's 'gnawing', but as a crucial step in the evolution of virtual space, and of Debord's *spectacle*. Bernard Comment makes a similar observation about the panorama (*Panorama*, p. 132).

35 Benjamin, 'The Work of Art in the Age of Mechanical Reproduction', p. 238.

13. Imaging

1 Greater London Industrial Archaeology Society Newsletter, February 2007, at glias.org.uk.

2 Karl-Artur Haag, at panoramio.com.

3 *Robinson in Ruins*, completed in 2010.

4 Adrian Rifkin, 'Benjamin's Paris, Freud's Rome: Whose London?', *Art History*, 22: 4 (1999), pp. 619–32.

5 The line connecting Stratford to the DLR at Canning Town opened in 2011.

6 Walter Benjamin, 'Surrealism: The Last Snapshot of the European Intelligentsia', in *One-Way Street*, pp. 225–39, at pp. 227, 229.

7 Christopher Phillips, ed., *Photography in the Modern Era: European Documents and Critical Writings 1913–1940* (New York: Metropolitan Museum of Art/ Aperture, 1989), p. 36.

8 Henri Lefebvre, *Critique of Everyday Life, Volume 1*, transl. John Moore (London/New York: Verso, 1991), pp. 103–29.

9 *Artists and Sound*, Tate Gallery, 23 August–19 September 1982.

10 Raoul Vaneigem, 'Self-Realisation, Communication and Participation' (Chapter 23 of *The Revolution of Everyday Life*) in *Leaving the Twentieth Century: The Incomplete Work of the Situationist International*, ed. and transl. Christopher Gray (London: Free Fall Publications, 1974), pp. 131–51.

11 Raoul Vaneigem, *The Revolution of Everyday Life*, transl. Donald Nicholson-Smith (Rebel Press/Left Bank Books, 1983, revised 1994), pp. 236–66.

12 Lefebvre, *Production of Space*, pp. 189–90. See also p. 142.

13 Henri Lefebvre, *Critique of Everyday Life, Volume 3*, transl. Gregory Elliott (London/New York: Verso, 1991), p. 57.

14 Lefebvre, *Critique of Everyday Life, Volume 1*, pp. 228–52, at p. 250.

15 Lefebvre, *Production of Space*, p. 25

16 Guillaume Apollinaire, *The False Amphion, or The Stories and Adventures of Baron d'Ormesan* in *The Heresiarch & Co.*, transl. Rémy Inglis Hall (Boston: Exact Change, 1991).

17 Roger Luckhurst, 'The Contemporary London Gothic and the Limits of the "Spectral Turn"', *Textual Practice* 16: 3 (2002), pp. 527–46.

Index